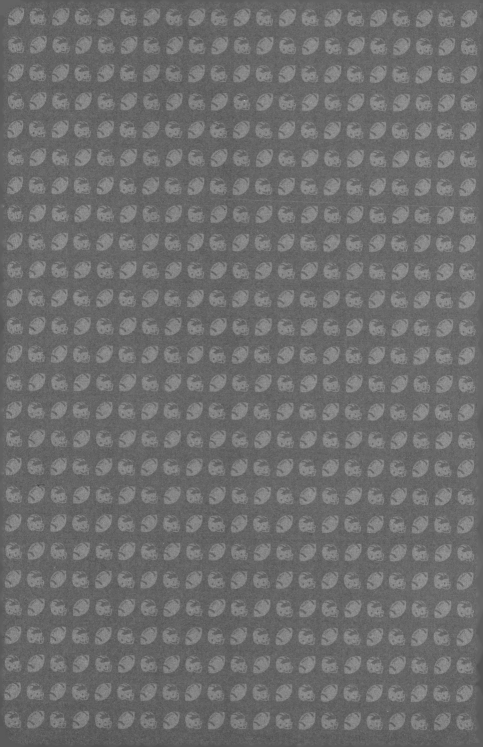

# A Gift For:

------------------------------------------------

# From:

------------------------------------------------

*Everything I do that's worth doing I dedicate to my one and only love, my wife Erica—you made these pages worth writing.*

Design by Alicia Freile and Gwen Galeone, Tango Media
Photographs courtesy of the Library of Congress
All illustrations courtesy of Shutterstock.com

ISBN: 978-1-59530-500-8
BOK4152

Printed and bound in China

# FOOTBALL

*The Players, The Records,*
*The Super Bowl*

## Ron Martirano

Kennebunkport, Maine

An early twentieth century gridiron practice

# ★ CONTENTS ★

----------------------------------

# Pregaming
# American Football

In the beginning, there was football. Two teams and a ball on whatever surface would have them. Variations of the game were played for centuries across Europe and beyond, exported like tea and war to fields of grass and dirt on every continent, including Antarctica.[1] The simplicity of the game and its equipment made it easily adaptable to every level of play, kicked or carried across oceans and class lines by immigrants and conquerors alike. Defend your territory while advancing upon an opponent's, coordinate your attacks with precision when possible, use brute force when necessary.

Modern football is more than a metaphor for life and aggression.[2] It is a hulking redwood with branches for legions of fans devoted to countless variations: English Premiere, World Cup, Rugby, Gaelic,

1 While there are no organized teams from Antarctica, a four-aside game was played there between scientists on September 21, 2009. Six men and four women battled it out in snowsuits in the name of world peace.

2 The "football as war" metaphor was turned on its head during World War I, during the unofficial "Christmas Truce" between English and German soldiers. Pleasantries and gifts were exchanged across the trenches, and one German soldier noted in his diary that a "lively game" of football was played. Germany lost the war, but they won the game 3-2.

Australian Rules, Canadian, and the American game among others. It is the source of fierce loyalty among and within its regions. There may be soccer in Green Bay and extra points attempted in London, but don't expect either to air at the local pub without a roll of the eyes from some of its patrons and downright revolt if they're broadcasted at the expense of the local game. It is also big business—International Federation of Association Football topped the billion-dollar revenue mark for the first time in 2009, and the National Football League (NFL) locked out its players in the summer of 2011 while still generating more than $8 billion. It is all of these things derived from sideshow beginnings—a traveling circus that came to town and never left.

*Rugby is a game for barbarians played by gentlemen. Football is a game for gentlemen played by barbarians.*

**—Oscar Wilde**

# Football Alumnus

## GRANTLAND RICE

*American appreciation for the "game of life" metaphors that football inspires led to one of its most-quoted verses, from preeminent sports writer Grantland Rice. Bill Jones's life on and off the field is football's answer to Casey's fabled at bat. The poem was originally recited with a final couplet at the end (and the words "writes" and "mark" transposed), but Rice knew a proper closing line when he saw it and edited the poem to its most celebrated conclusion.*

Bill Jones had been the shining star upon his college team;
His tackling was ferocious and his bucking was a dream;
When husky William took the ball beneath this brawny arm
They kept a special man to ring the ambulance alarm.

Bill hit the line and ran the ends like some mad bull amuck;
The other team would shiver when they saw him start to buck;
And when the rival forwards tried to stand him on his head
The coaches called an armistice and put away their dead.

Bill had the weight. Bill had the speed—the nerve to never yield;
They called him "Siege Gun Willie" as he shrapneled down the field,
For there had been a standing bet (which no one tried to call)
That Bill could make his distance through a ten-foot granite wall.

## Chapter Two.

When he wound up his college course each student's heart was sore;
They wept to think that husky Bill would hit the line no more.
Not so with William—in his dreams he saw the Field of Fame,
Where he would buck to glory in the swirl of Life's big game.

So with his sheepskin tucked beneath his brawny arm, one day
Bill put on steam and dashed into the thickest of the fray;
With eyes ablaze he sprinted where the laurelled highway led;
When Bill woke up his scalp hung loose and knots adorned his head.

He tried to skirt the Ends of Life but lo, with vicious toss,
A bill collector tackled him and threw him for a loss;
And when he switched his course again and crashed into the line,
The massive guard named Failure did a tango on his spine.

Bill tried to punt out of the rut, but ere he turned the trick
Right Tackle Competition tumbled through and blocked the kick;
And when he tacked at Success in one long vicious bound,
The fullback Disappointment steered his features in the ground.

## Chapter Three.

But one day, when across the Field of Fame the goal seemed dim,
The wise old coach Experience came up and spoke to him.
"Old top," he said, "the main point is before you win your bout
To keep on bucking Failure till you've warn that piker out.

"Cut out this stuff around the ends; go in there low and hard;
Forget all this New Football as you move on yard by yard;
And more than all, when you are thrown or tumbled with a crack,
Don't lie there whining, hustle up, and keep on coming back.

"Keep coming back with all you've got and take it with a grin
When Disappointment trips you up and Failure barks your shin;
Keep coming back, and say to Fate, the while her minions gloat;
'Come on and take my shirt and hat, but you can't get my goat.'

"Keep coming back, and though the world may romp across your map,
Let every scrimmage find you still somewhere within the scrap;
>    For when the One Great Scorer comes
>    To mark against your name,
>    He writes—not that you won or lost—
>    But HOW you played the Game."

The grandfather of all games may have been *harpaston,* a brutal contest played by the ancient Greeks with one objective—get the ball across the goal line. Varied forms were played for the next millennia, brutality being the common thread among them all as the end of the match generally coincided with the beginning of the brawl that inevitably followed. Football is mostly credited to the English public schools of the early nineteenth century (hereon referred to as "soccer" to illustrate the author's bias toward the U.S. reader and his willingness to antagonize everyone else[3]). The soccer played at Eton and Winchester in the 1800s closely resembles the game today, but one English school took a different approach to the rules—at Rugby School they picked up the ball and ran with it.

American football has its strongest and most obvious roots in rugby. Beyond the ability to use one's hands, both games have their version of goal posts that can be kicked over for points. The first recognized American game was played between Princeton and Rutgers on November 6, 1869. Using modified London Football Association rules, the game inspired a following that would forever divert the interests of the country away from the soccer rules used elsewhere. While its following was growing, the game as it was played was still too violent and unorganized for official acceptance. When it began to take further root in the Ivy League universities, its survival depended on the adoption of rules to distinguish it from the melee it was often mistaken for.

The Intercollegiate Football Association (IFA) was formed in 1876 in an attempt to legitimize and standardize the game. Columbia, Rutgers, Princeton, and Yale University had members on hand at the group's first meeting in New York City. It was Yale coach Walter Camp who would

3 The name *soccer* is believed to come from the shortening of Association Football.

emerge from the IFA as the father of American football. What Alexander Cartwright was to baseball, Camp was to football (see the Appendix for examples of Camp's original writing on the game). He successfully lobbied for 11-man teams and formalized the playing field. In the years that followed, Camp would introduce the snap from center as the catalyst to play. He would also establish the original line of scrimmage as well as the yardage and downs necessary for advancement (originally five yards over three downs before being adjusted to today's standard).

Walter Camp had begun the process of fully distinguishing American football from its global counterparts, and while further rule changes would continue for the next century, there was still one key movement to be made for football to become football. Many still believed the sport was too violent—and with good reason. Within a decade of organized play, the game had already resulted in 18 deaths and almost 180 serious injuries. The call to ban football from American campuses had already been answered at some colleges, and greater sanctions were on the horizon. *Collier's Weekly* even ran an editorial in support of canceling the annual Harvard–Yale game unless changes were made, arguing that the "greater Universities" were setting a bad example for the rest of the nation. The sport needed to be saved from itself. Enter Teddy Roosevelt.

*In life, as in a football game, the principle to follow is: Hit the line hard.*

—**Theodore Roosevelt**

# "The Case against Football"

— from *Collier's Weekly*, March 1903

A member of the Harvard faculty who has been connected with the athletic committee of the university has caused a great deal of discussion by suggesting the advisability of discontinuing the annual Harvard–Yale football game. The reasons he gives are that the contest has become too exciting both to undergraduates and graduates, that it upsets the serious work of the students and creates unworthy antagonism between the universities, and that football as it is now played is too dangerous to life and limb. Of course these statements have been disputes and Mr. Hollis has been widely denounced as a spoil-sport, but we think the general opinion of the country is that the time has arrived for the university authorities to take action in this matter. The game of football long ago ceased to be a form of healthful recreation. At present it is a source of unwholesome rivalry to the students and a spectacle of uncivilized ferocity to the general public. Merely as a spectacle it has lost nearly all the features that appeal to a healthy love of sport. If the spectator were unaware of the depth and intensity of the rivalry it is doubtful whether he could see anything properly amusing in the pushing and slugging that carries the ball down the field. But that is beside the question. The chief complaint we have to make against intercollegiate football relates to its effect beyond the walls of the university. Rugby football will always be played by small colleges and schools as it is played in the great universities. Harvard and Yale practically dictate the rules for the country. If they play fiercely, encourage crushing "formations" and minimize the rewards of agility and presence of mind, the small fry will follow their example. Their well-trained men may be temporarily disabled by a play which will kill a half-grown youth. The rushing that knocks the breath out of a Harvard centre may knock the life out of a high-school boy. No one in the great universities has been killed or crippled by the brutal plays now practiced, but year by year the list of fatalities among the teams of the small colleges and schools grows. As we have said once before, the athletic committees of the universities are the stewards of the game in this country, and it is their duty either to abolish the contests or to so modify the rules that the sport will cease to be dangerous to the lives of the players. It is time the faculties took the decisions out of the hands of the impulsive politicians of athletics among the undergraduates and the conservative statesmen among the graduate coaches and gave this matter the treatment which its public importance demands.

In 1905, at President Roosevelt's prompting,[4] sixty schools gathered to form a Rules Committee—the precursor to the National Collegiate Athletic Association (NCAA). The committee believed that the greatest safety threats within the game were the collisions caused by too many bodies playing too closely together. They needed to open up the field and create greater natural distance between players. The outlawing of locked-arm formations and establishment of a neutral zone at the start of each play were both steps in the right direction. Cutting the game down from seventy minutes to sixty would further limit the chance of injury. But two innovations would come out of the committee that would complete the creation of the American game as we know it—the institution of the forward pass and the redesign of the ball so it could be properly thrown.

While the game's on-field identity was fully coming together, it had already spread from coast to coast finding eager participants not only in colleges across the heartland but in amateur athletic clubs as well. Intense rivalries flared between local teams, even with attending crowds measuring only in the hundreds. In Pittsburgh, the Allegheny Athletic Association (AAA) and the Pittsburgh Athletic Club were two such rivals who brought upon the next evolution of the sport. The November 12, 1892, game between them was a 32-0 blowout for the Allegheny. Overshadowing the final score was William "Pudge" Heffelfinger. A former Yale All-American guard, Heffelfinger had received the then-exorbitant sum of $500 to play for AAA. Not only did he recover a fumble and return it 35 yards for a touchdown, but he also became the first player in the history of the game to get paid to do so. Standing at the head of a line that would one day see $100 million contracts and beyond, the professional football player had entered the game.

4 Some would say "prompting" while others would say "threat to have the game banned."

# 1896–1932

For much of the public, professional football was a novelty at best in its earliest days. Teams comprised of pay-for-play players had followed Allegheny's example, but several attempts to organize under common rules had folded early. One such attempt was the original National Football League, a short-lived venture that included Philadelphia Athletics manager/owner Connie Mack as one of its founders. The first NFL shared other ties to its professional baseball counterpart; Mack's team, also the Athletics, featured future hall-of-famer Rube Waddell, while the legendary hall-of-famer Christy Matthewson played fullback for the Pittsburgh Stars. Teams met in a post-season World Series of pro football, a five-team tournament first played in New York City at the original Madison Square Garden. The tourney saw mixing and matching of existing clubs to field the full bracket and give New Yorkers a home team to root for, but it only made it through two seasons. The first professional football league championship was won by a Syracuse Athletic Club team with Glenn Scobey "Pop" Warner at offensive guard, the second by the Franklin Pennsylvania Athletic Club.

Following the original NFL's demise, pro teams popped up around the country, playing through barnstorming seasons against an unorganized schedule of ragtag, municipal, and sometimes company/factory-owned teams. The game and its rules continued to evolve over this twenty-year stretch just as the college game had before it, with changes to scoring values—field goals dropped from five, to four, and eventually three points, while touchdowns rose from four points to their current worth. Several strong teams emerged, including the Canton Bulldogs, featuring Jim Thorpe as both star player and coach. Thorpe was one of the most celebrated athletes of his day, having gained fame for winning the decathlon and pentathlon at the 1912 Olympics, only to have his medals stripped for having previously played professional minor-league baseball.[5] Other noteworthy teams included the Morgan Athletic Club from Chicago's south side and Curly Lambeau's Green Bay Packers. All they needed was a legitimate, structured league to showcase their talents.

In 1920 the American Professional Football Conference (APFC) was founded in the showroom of a car dealership in Canton, Ohio. At the time, Ohio was already a hotbed for budding pro teams, and four teams from the Buckeye State made up the original league roster—the Akron Pros, Canton Bulldogs, Cleveland Indians, and Dayton Triangles. A month later the roster expanded beyond the state lines to include the Hammond Pros, Rochester Jeffersons, Rock Island Independents, and Muncie Flyers. Also among the new teams were the former Morgan Athletic Club, now called the Chicago Cardinals, and the Decatur Staleys.

Renamed the American Professional Football Association (APFA), the most glaring flaw in the early league's structure was that there was no schedule to build a season around. Games could be played against any number of teams—both in and outside the league. Jim Thorpe was elected president, but it was a move made to give the league name recognition,

---

5 Thorpe would also go on to play Major League Baseball for the Giants, Reds, and Braves. His Olympic medals were restored posthumously.

not leadership. Along the way, the league roster for the inaugural season was completed with the inclusion of four additional teams[6]: the Columbus Panhandles, Chicago Tigers, Detroit Heralds, and Buffalo All-Americans.

The big game that pro football would become didn't even have a big game to hinge its seasons on. The first thirteen league champions (official and otherwise) weren't crowned on the field but were determined by a committee—the uneven, unbalanced schedule making winning percentage the best available measure of greatness. The 1920 Akron Pros finished the kickoff season undefeated, with eight wins and a tie, and although the Staleys had two additional wins, their 10-1-2 record was only good enough for second place, as the Pros were considered (but never officially awarded the title) first league champions. The Staleys were the company team of the A. E. Staley Corn Products Company and run by a former halfback from the University of Illinois and one-time Yankee call-up by the name of George Halas. Unfortunately, the company could not afford to maintain a department's worth of employees whose daily work in the mill included two-hour practice sessions. A year after their inaugural kickoff, Halas would take over and move them to Chicago. Staley gave him $5,000 to help with the transition and only asked that the team keep the Staley name for an additional season. Staley's investment paid off, as Halas's team would make it to the unglamorous promised land as unofficial league champions in its final year playing under the Staley banner. In a tip-of-the-hat move to the second city's premiere baseball franchise, he would rename his team the Bears.

From the beginning, Halas had installed himself as a significant feature in how the league was run, and he would go on to have great impact

6 All four teams would play against other APFA/NFL opponents and be included in league standings going forward, but their official status as league members in 1920 is the subject of debate.

on its development. He had already launched a successful campaign to have Thorpe replaced as president following the 1920 season. Halas was reportedly bitter that his claim to the 1920 title was not recognized, as by his perspective the Staleys had more wins and had tied Akron in a scoreless affair to end the season. His support of new league president Joe Carr (who ran the Columbus team) led to official recordkeeping and an advocate in the head office. Halas's influence further demonstrated itself in the offseason following the Staleys' first title, as he lobbied to have the league's name changed. Beginning the 1922 season, professional football in America would be played in the National Football League.

The league's first decade was a tumultuous one, as the organization was in many ways a work in progress. None of the original teams outside of the Bears and Cardinals made it to the 1930s, but in the interim the NFL would survive a challenge from a rival league and admit over a half-dozen new teams to expand its presence, among them stalwarts like Lambeau's Green Bay Packers and Tim Mara's New York Giants. The remainder of the decade would see first-title honors for both teams, as well as the Cardinals—now the longest continually run professional franchise going back to its independent seasons. The 1920s also saw the emergence of the NFL's first marquee player, Red Grange—the "Galloping Ghost."

As professional football entered its second decade, one element was still missing—a championship game. After three consecutive Green Bay titles, the Packers were poised for number four in 1932 before being overrun by the Portland Steamroller, a defector from the AFL. Portland was positioned to take the title had Green Bay won its final game of the season, but the Pack lost to Chicago, setting up a playoff for the championship. As much as Halas and the Bears wanted a second title for their mantel, what the team really needed was a large enough draw to cover the season's expenses. With temperatures hovering around the zero mark and Wrigley Field frozen solid, there was no way the game would pull in a paying crowd big enough to pay off everyone involved. On short notice the title match was moved indoors to Chicago Stadium. The field was short in every dimension; it could accommodate punts but not field goals, and kickoffs needed to be made from the 10-yard line, but it was enough for $15,000 in gate receipts and, following a Bronko Nagurski pass to Red Grange and a safety, a Bears win.

The era of the big game was about to begin.

*This man Red Grange of Illinois is three or four men rolled into one for football purposes… He is Jack Dempsey, Babe Ruth, Al Jolson, Paavo Nurmi and Man o' War. Put together, they spell Grange.*

**—Damon Runyon**

# RED GRANGE:
## The Galloping Ghost

Babe Ruth may have been the man responsible for the original Yankee Stadium being built, but Red Grange—professional football's first superstar—required his own New York Yankee team to house his stardom. Grantland Rice is usually credited with giving Grange the nickname "Galloping Ghost," on account of his elusive presence once he got his hands on the ball; however, Grange himself claimed Chicago American sportswriter Warren Brown gave him his famous moniker. Harold "Red" Grange was already a celebrity at the University of Illinois, his college career headlined by a devastating performance against the University of Michigan that included a 95-yard kickoff return and touchdown runs of 67, 56, and 44 yards—all in the first 12 minutes of play! He came back in the second half with another touchdown run (11 yards) and a 20-yard touchdown pass. He saw himself on the cover of *Time* magazine as a senior and finished the season leading the Illini to victory over Ohio State during a controversial recruitment to the NFL—he was signed, sealed, and delivered to the Bears within a week, in time to play in Chicago's Thanksgiving game.

The Galloping Ghost would finish out Chicago's season and then embark on a breakneck tour of the country, playing to massive crowds everywhere he went. His professional debut in New York is credited with saving the Giants as a franchise, as 73,000 came to see him at the Polo Grounds. Weeks later he enticed similar numbers to Los Angeles Memorial Coliseum. All in all, the Galloping Ghost had played 19 games in less than two months and earned more than $200,000. He was such a draw that the following season his manager, Charles Pyle, sought partial ownership of the Bears in exchange for his continued play. When Halas refused, Pyle launched his own football league, the American Football League (AFL), with Red Grange as the marquee name for its New York franchise—the Yankees.

The new league, sometimes referred to as the Grange League or the AFLG, did not last long. With the Galloping Ghost's Yankees as the only real draw, most of the teams folded after a year (including the league champion Philadelphia Quakers, who finished the season 8-2). Grange rejoined the NFL in 1927 and he took his Yankees with him, taking the place of the Brooklyn Lions, who had joined the league the previous season. While Grange had racked up fame and endorsements (everything from dolls, sweaters, and shoes to candy bars, soft drinks, and even meat loaf), he also began to feel the effect of his grueling schedule in the form of injuries. After twisting his ankle in a game against the Bears, Grange called it quits and embarked on a brief movie career before realizing that if he was well enough to perform his own stunts, he was well enough to play. By now the Yankees were no more, leading to Grange's reunion with Halas and the Bears—a relationship that would last for six more seasons on the field. In that time, Grange and the Bears would take home titles in 1932 and 1933. The 1933 championship was the first to be determined by a scheduled championship game, and it was Grange who saved it for Chicago with a late fourth-quarter tackle to prevent the Giants from scoring a go-ahead touchdown. Following his playing career, he would stay with the Bears as an assistant coach before moving over to the broadcast booth, where he covered the team for fourteen years. Halas would later say of him that "no player had a greater impact on the game of football, college or professional, than Grange." In 1963 he was inducted into the Pro Football Hall of Fame's inaugural class.

# ARIZONA CARDINALS

*Chicago Cardinals (1920–1943, 1945–1959);*
*Chi/Pitt Cards/Steelers (1945); St. Louis Cardinals*
*(1960–1987); Phoenix Cardinals (1988–1993)*

*Founded* 1920

*Ring of Honor*
Charles Bidwill, Ernie Nevers, Jimmy Conzelman,
John "Paddy" Driscoll, Charley Trippi, Ollie Matson, Dick "Night
Train" Lane, Marshall Goldberg, Dan Dierdorf, Pat Tillman,
Larry Wilson, Roger Wehrli, Aeneas Williams

*Retired Numbers*
8—Larry Wilson; 40—Pat Tillman; 77—Stan Mauldin;
88—J. V. Cain; 99—Marshall Goldberg

*Division/Conference Championships* 3: 1947, 1948, 2008

*NFL Championships* 1: 1947

---

## THE RECORDS

Three players share the record for most receiving touchdowns
in a game (5): Bob Shaw (Cardinals), Kellen Winslow (Chargers),
and Jerry Rice (49ers).

---

The Cards are generally recognized as the oldest-running professional football franchise, with its roots going back to the Morgan Athletic Club of 1898. They were a charter member of the AFPA. Their first title was a controversial win over the Pottsville Maroons, in which one of their opponents was discovered to have fielded high school players. The team changed hands several times in its early years, ending up with Chicago Bears' part-owner Charles Bidwill, who put in place an agreement with his former partner George Halas that divided the city at Madison Street—the Bears took the north side and the Cards took the South.

The Cardinals were one of several teams to temporarily merge during World War II, taking the field as part of a Cardinals/Steelers hybrid team in 1945. The team had its first real on-field success after the war, beating the Eagles in their first championship game in 1947. They played and lost in the final the following year, and thereafter went into a decline that included the loss of an argument with the crosstown rival Bears over their plans to move into a bigger stadium north of the agreed-upon dividing line. Fortunately, while the league sided against the Cardinals in their efforts to move across town, they were willing (and pressured by broadcast partner CBS) to subsidize the team's move to St. Louis so they could skirt around the television blackout rules of the day. The Cardinals of the sporting world were aligned at Busch Stadium for almost thirty years, an unmemorable stretch that produced a single playoff game victory and ended when the team packed its bags for Phoenix. The Arizona née Phoenix Cardinals got a brief taste of the good life in 2008 when a resurgent Kurt Warner led the team to an appearance in Super Bowl XLIII.

# CHICAGO BEARS

*Decatur Staleys (1920); Chicago Staleys (1921)*

*Founded* 1920

*Retired Numbers*

3—Bronko Nagurski; 5—George McAfee; 7—George Halas;
28—Willie Galimore; 34—Walter Payton; 40—Gale Sayers;
41—Brian Piccolo; 42—Sid Luckman; 51—Dick Butkus;
56—Bill Hewitt; 61—Bill George; 66—Bulldog Turner;
77—Red Grange

*Division/Conference Championships*

12: 1933, 1934, 1937, 1940, 1941, 1942, 1943, 1946,
1956, 1963, 1985, 2006

*NFL Championships/Super Bowl Victories*

9: 1921, 1932, 1933, 1940, 1941, 1943, 1946, 1963,
Super Bowl XX (1985)

The "Monsters of the Midway" were designed, created, owned, and coached by George "Papa Bear" Halas. Halas's Bears were a charter team in the APFA and most influential in its development. Decked out in navy and orange in honor of Halas's alma mater, the University of Illinois, the Bears signed the league's first superstar and won its first championship game. A perennial contender before World War II, the Bears went on a dominant run behind quarterback Sid Luckman and the then-radical T-formation offense in the 1940s that earned them their monstrous nickname.

The postwar teams did not enjoy the successes of their predecessors, but Halas would see one more title before ceding sideline control in 1967. That last title came in 1963 with Billy Wade at QB and Mike Ditka at tight end. It would be more than twenty years later, two years after the Papa Bear passed away, that the Bears would make a bid to restore the franchise with one of the most dominant teams to play in the modern age. With Ditka returned to the franchise as head coach, the 1985 Bears went 15-1 and stormed through the playoffs, allowing only 10 total points in three games to win their only Super Bowl.

# DAYTON TRIANGLES

*Seasons Played in the APFA/NFL* 1920–1929

*Lifetime Record* 18-51-8

*Best Season Finish* 1920, sixth place (5-2-2)

On October 3, 1920, the Dayton Triangles played and won the very first APFA game, defeating the Columbus Panhandles 14-0. Dayton's first season was its most successful, with its only two losses coming against league champion Akron. Dayton avoided playing losing football for the next two seasons but soon declined to the point where from 1923–1929 they only won five games (with no wins in 1925, 1928, and 1929, respectively). The team ended its run in Dayton after the 1929 season, when it was sold and moved to Brooklyn.

# HAMMOND PROS

*Seasons Played in the APFA/NFL* 1920–1926

*Lifetime Record[7]* 7-28-4

*Best Season Finish*

1920, 1924—eleventh place (1920: 2-5, statistically tied with Chicago Tigers, 2-5-1, as tied games were not considered for the standings at that time; 1924: 2-2-1)

The Pros' best season was 1924, when they finished .500 with 2 wins, 2 losses, and a tie (by the old NFL standing rules, tie games had no statistical value and were treated as if they had not been played). They never won more than two games in a season, never scored more points than they allowed, and hold a distinction in futility by being completely shut out on offense for the 1922 season, going 0-5-1 on the year. They disbanded following the 1926 season, when they went 0-4 with 3 points scored on the year.

---

7 Lifetime records for inactive franchises include all scheduled games played after 1920, including those against non-league opponents.

# BUFFALO ALL-AMERICANS/ BUFFALO BISONS

*Seasons Played in the APFA/NFL* 1920–1927, 1929

*Lifetime Record* 40-37-12

*Best Season Finish* 1921, second place (9-1-2)

The All-Americans were a fixture in the APFA standings from the beginning. The team took shape prior to World War I and played its way into the new league, challenging its way to the top spot on the leaderboard until the final game of the 1920 season, when a loss to Akron dropped them down to third. They were again in contention in 1921 until it was discovered that Buffalo players were moonlighting for a Philadelphia independent team on Saturdays (Pennsylvania blue laws prevented the Philly teams from taking part in Sunday games). Offending players were forced to choose between the two, and defections led to several replacement players being added to the roster. The team had been undefeated up until that point, and while the substitutes faired well, they lost the final game of the season to Decatur. At 9-1-2, the practice of disregarding ties should have worked in their favor when deciding the 1921 league champion, but the 9-1 Staleys were awarded the title.

The team changed their name to the Bisons in 1924. Sadly, the practice of referring to the plural of "Bison" as "Bisons" in Buffalo is part of a multisport tradition of grammatical failure that goes back to the 1800s—the original Bisons played in baseball's

National League during the nineteenth century and have resurfaced in various incarnations since, including the current AAA team. The football Bisons were briefly renamed the Rangers in 1926, returned as the Bisons in 1927, failed to play in 1928, and took to the field for one final season in 1929 before disbanding.

-----------------------

# COLUMBUS PANHANDLES/ COLUMBUS TIGERS

*Seasons Played in the APFA/NFL* 1920–1926

*Lifetime Record* 13-45-3

*Best Season Finish* 1923, eighth place (5-4-1)

Columbus's team is included with the original charter teams, although the details of its actual admission to the league are uncertain. Still, the team played a regular schedule against NFL opponents and in fact took part in the first NFL game, getting shut out by Dayton. The relationship between the Panhandles and the Tigers is equally unclear, but both teams are generally viewed as one and the same, and if nothing else, Columbus had its best and only non-losing seasons under the Tigers banner. The non-failure was brief, as the 1925 team went 0-9 and the franchise would win only one more game before folding, going 1-6 in 1926.

# CANTON BULLDOGS

*Seasons Played in the APFA/NFL*
1920–1923, 1925–1926

*Lifetime Record* 38-19-11

*Championship Seasons* 1922 (10-0-2), 1923 (11-0-1)

---

### THE RECORDS

From 1921 through 1923, the Canton Bulldogs went on a 25-game run that set a still-standing record for the most consecutive games without a defeat. Over that period they were 22-0-3.

---

An Ohio League fixture and NFL charter member, the Bulldogs enjoyed some success on both sides of their NFL membership. With Jim Thorpe as their star player and coach, they took home three Ohio League Championships from 1916 to 1919 (they sat out the 1918 season on account of World War I) before taking position in the APFA with the other charter teams. The Bulldogs took home two NFL championships before they were purchased and moved to Cleveland in 1924. At the end of the 1924 season, the team was sold again and moved back to Canton, where they played two final seasons before disbanding. Their proximity to the league's founding meeting and the current hall of fame has given them some staying power. Today, their Facebook page proudly displays the "World Champions 1922" banner.

# AKRON PROS/AKRON INDIANS

*Seasons Played in the APFA/NFL* 1920–1926

*Lifetime Record* 27-26-11

*Championships* 1920 (8-0-3)

A charter team of the APFA and the league's first champion, the Pros managed 16 wins against 3 losses in their first two years of play. They maintain the distinction of having hired the league's first black coach, taking former Brown University All-American halfback Fritz Pollard as a co-coach for their 8-3-1 1921 season. After the APFA became the NFL, things did not fare as well for the Akron team, which had losing seasons in three of their next four seasons. A name-change to the Indians in 1926 did not improve the team's fortune; they finished the year at 1-4-3 before folding.

# ROCHESTER JEFFERSONS

*Seasons Played in the APFA/NFL* 1920–1925

*Lifetime Record* 8-27-4

*Best Season Finish* 1920, seventh place (6-3-2)

Rochester's club managed several years of local success before making the trip to Canton to sign on with the APFA charter. Their first season in the league was their most successful, as they won only two games the following year and did not manage another win in their final four years of existence.

# ROCK ISLAND INDEPENDENTS

*Seasons Played in the APFA/NFL* 1920–1925

*Season Played in the AFL* 1926

*Lifetime NFL Record* 26-14-12

*Lifetime AFL Record* 2-6-1

*Best NFL Season Finish*
1920, fourth place (6-2-2, tied with Chicago Cardinals)

*AFL Season Finish* seventh place

The Rock Island Independents out of the Tri-Cities region of Illinois bear the distinction of being the only professional football team to sit as a charter member of both the APFA/NFL and Red Grange's AFL. The team finished all but one of its APFA/NFL seasons with a winning record but suffered financially after jumping ship to join the new league in 1926 and never recovered, folding the following season.

# DETROIT HERALDS/
# DETROIT TIGERS

*Seasons Played in the APFA* 1920–1921

*Lifetime Record* 3-8-4

*Best Season Finish* 1920, ninth place (2-3-3)

The Heralds' history goes back to 1905, when the team formed as an amateur squad of University of Detroit players who wanted to keep playing even though the college could not afford to fund the team. They would keep the team going for the next fifteen years as an independent, and eventually semi-pro, organization before becoming affiliated with the APFA. The Heralds had only two wins in their inaugural season. They gave it one more try in 1921, regrouping as the Tigers. Detroit scored 19 points on the season, winning a single game on the year. Lack of payment forced the team to disband before they could finish out their schedule.

# CLEVELAND TIGERS/ CLEVELAND INDIANS

*Seasons Played in the APFA* 1920–1921

*Lifetime Record* 5-9-2

*Best Season Finish* 1920, tenth place (2-4-2)

The Tigers were a charter team in 1920 and managed one win on the season. They regrouped as the Indians in 1921 and brought on Jim Thorpe as a player/coach. The reconstituted Tribe improved on the previous year but would ultimately prove to be no luckier in football than they were in baseball, as Cleveland finished 3-5 on the season before calling it quits as a franchise.

# MUNCIE FLYERS

*Seasons Played in the APFA* 1920–1921

*Lifetime Record* 0-3

*Best Season Finish* 1920, fourteenth place (0-1)

After ten years of semi-professional play, Muncie, Indiana's charter APFA team, got off to a rocky start in the league and never recovered. Shutout 45-0 in their first game of the 1920 season, they were seen as such a poor draw that they could not get another league member to play against them that year (Decatur canceled what would have been their Week 2 matchup). They finished the season, and ultimately their professional existence, both winless and scoreless—0-1 in 1920 and 0-2 in 1921. With no one willing to take an easy win in exchange for a poor gate, they folded after the 1921 season.

# CHICAGO TIGERS

*Season Played in the APFA* 1920

*Lifetime Record* 2-5-1

*Season Finish*
eleventh place (statistically tied with Hammond Pros, 2-5, as tied
games were not considered for the standings at that time)

Chicago's single year of play in the APFA was so uneventful that
some question whether they were ever officially a part of the league.
Whether they were documented members or not, the team played a
full schedule against the rest of the league, finishing tied for eleventh
in the standings at 2-5-1 (twelfeth by today's standards). Of their two
victories, one was against the Detroit Heralds, the other against an
independent Chicago team—the Thorn Tornadoes.

# GREEN BAY PACKERS

*Founded* 1921

### *Retired Numbers*
3—Tony Canadeo; 14—Don Hutson; 15—Bart Starr;
66—Ray Nitschke; 92—Reggie White

### *Conference Championships*
13: 1936, 1938, 1939, 1944, 1960, 1961, 1962, 1965, 1966,
1967, 1996, 1997, 2010

### *NFL Championships/Super Bowl Victories*
13: 1929, 1930, 1931, 1936, 1939, 1944, 1961, 1962, 1965,
Super Bowl I (1966), Super Bowl II (1967), Super Bowl XXXI (1996),
Super Bowl XLV (2010)

---

### THE RECORDS
The Green Bay Packers hold the record for league
championships, at 13.

---

The Packers' roots go back to 1919, but the team didn't join the APFA/
NFL until 1921. The team was named for the Acme Packing Company.
After a scandal involving college players, the team was sold back to
the league and resold to Curly Lambeau, who in turn was forced to
set the team up as a public non-profit corporation—the only profes-

sional franchise of its kind still in operation today. Lambeau stayed on as general manager and coach, and led the team to six titles before departing in 1950.

Over the next decade the Packers wouldn't see much success in the standings, but they would define the franchise with an iconic stadium—City Stadium, later renamed Lambeau Field—and an iconic coach, Vince Lombardi. Lombardi would lift the team to greatness. With players such as Bart Starr and the "Golden Boy" Paul Hornung, Green Bay would produce winning seasons in each of Lombardi's nine seasons, including back-to-back championships. Titletown USA was born and its dynasty team would see a second run, with three consecutive titles—including victories in the first two Super Bowls. Lombardi stepped down after Super Bowl II and eventually departed to coach in Washington. The team slipped into its longest stretch of poor play, staying out of the regular playoff picture until Brett Favre and coach Mike Holmgren brought another title to Titletown almost thirty years later.

*The difference between a successful person and others is not lack of strength, not lack of knowledge, but rather a lack of will.*

**—Vince Lombardi**

# MINNEAPOLIS MARINES/
# MINNEAPOLIS RED JACKETS

*Seasons Played in the APFA/NFL*

1921–1924, 1929–1930

*Lifetime Record* 6-33-3

*Best Season* 1930, tenth place (1-7-1)

The Minneapolis Marines are the epitome of a homegrown team, having originated as a youth squad. The all-amateur bunch began playing together in 1905 as part of an under-115 pound league, before literally growing up together on the field into the team that won the 1910 city championship. Eventually, outsiders were allowed in, and within a decade the team's schedule moved beyond the city's borders. The Marines joined the APFA in 1921, scattering four wins across four seasons before folding in 1924. In 1929, ownership gave it another shot, calling the team the Red Jackets (a tribute to the Marines' red uniforms), and put in two more seasons of play. The Red Jackets fared no better than their predecessors, averaging a win a season for two years before leaving the league for good.

# LOUISVILLE BRECKS/
# LOUISVILLE COLONELS

*Seasons Played in the APFA/NFL*
1921–1923, 1926

*Lifetime Record* 1-12

*Best Season*
1922, thirteenth place (1-3, tied with the Minneapolis Marines)

Named for Breckinridge Street, on which their original field was located, the Brecks' inglorious history has its highlight in a single victory against the Evansville Crimson Giants in 1922. In four years of play, the 13-6 win against Evansville would mark the only occasion in which the Brecks scored points. In fact, 1923 should have been their last season in the NFL, but a lifetime professional record of 1-8 and being outscored by a combined 244 points was enough to warrant concern that the team would catch on in the emerging AFL three years later. Rather than risk the competition, the league invited them back for the 1926 season. Playing as the Colonels, Louisville was a road team. They went 0-4 and were shut out on offense 108-0.

# EVANSVILLE CRIMSON GIANTS

## *Seasons Played in the APFA/NFL*
1921–1922

## *Lifetime Record* 3-5

## *Best Season* 1921, sixth place (3-2)

This two-year operation joined the APFA in 1921 and finished the season with a 3-2 record. While the sixth-place finish made for a stronger showing than most of the other short-history franchises, the three wins came against lowest-rung opponents. The following year when the league became the NFL, the Crimson Giants went 0-3.

# WASHINGTON SENATORS

*Season Played in the APFA* 1921

*Lifetime Record* 1-2

*Season Finish* twelfth place

First in war and last in the AFPA? Not these Senators. Washington's twelfth-place finish in their only season of existence put them pretty much in the middle of the 21-team pack. Some accounts of their lone season even improve upon their 1-2 record by adding a win courtesy of a Rochester Jeffersons forfeit (the Jeffersons supposedly couldn't afford to make the trip). Whether they were a .500 team or a .333 team in 1921, it became their lifetime record, as the Senators folded at the end of the season.

# TONAWANDA KARDEX

*Season Played in the APFA* 1921

*Lifetime Record* 0-1

*Season Finish* eighteenth place

The Tonawanda Kardex were shutout 45-0 by the Rochester Jeffersons in 1921. That is as much as can be said about the one-season professional history of the corporate team of American Kardex, a producer of card index systems still in operation today as Remington Rand. The Lumbermen (as they were also known) played on a high school field in a small upstate New York town located between Buffalo and Niagara Falls. They originated as a regional all-star team and had won the 1917 New York Pro Football league's state championship before joining the APFA.

# NEW YORK BRICKLEY GIANTS

*Season Played in the APFA* 1921

*Lifetime Record* 0-2

*Season Finish* eighteenth place[8]

The New York Brickley Giants were at one point in their pre-APFA history backed by baseball's Giants, with Harvard's All-American half-back Charles Brickley slotted to run the team. A misunderstanding of how New York's blue laws would apply to football kept the team from taking the field in the year of its formation, 1919. Two years later, Sunday football was officially on the books in New York and the franchise was invited into the APFA. Unfortunately, New York failed to realize that being allowed to play on Sunday would include playing on offense (or defense for that matter), as the Giants fell 55-0 in their opening game against Buffalo and 17-0 a month later versus Cleveland, with no other league games in between. The team did not participate in the 1922 season and disbanded shortly thereafter.

---

8 With four "defeated teams" in 1921, the Giants were statistically tied for eighteenth/last place in the league; however, their points differential of -72 was by far the worst among the three 0-2 teams, putting them in last among the last. If one team had to get the honor of having the single-worst lifetime record in the APFA/NFL, the Brickley Giants would need to be considered the strongest of contenders.

# CINCINNATI CELTS

*Season Played in the APFA* 1921

*Lifetime Record* 1-3

*Season Finish* thirteenth place

Another one-and-done franchise, the feast-or-famine Celts played four games in 1921. They were shut out 41-0 by Akron, 28-0 by Cleveland, and 48-0 by the Evansville Crimson Giants. In between, they perpetrated a shutout of their own against the Muncie Flyers, the franchise's lone victory.

# MILWAUKEE BADGERS

*Seasons Played in the NFL*
1922–1926

*Lifetime Record* 16-27-6

*Best Season* 1923, fourth place (7-2)

The Badgers came in to the NFL in 1922 and had one strong season and one unusual controversy to mark their five-year existence. Their 7-2 record was good enough for fourth place in 1923, but it did nothing for attendance, and the team declined over the next two years. The 1925 team was 0-5 with only seven points scored on the year when the team began disbanding. Across the league, the Chicago Cardinals needed additional wins to overtake the Pottsville Maroons for first place. Pottsville had just defeated Chicago the previous Sunday and statistically was one win ahead for the league title. A game against Milwaukee was scheduled for that Thursday, and the Badgers filled their missing roster slots with high school players—either to help Chicago out or simply on account of the logistical issues with reassembling the team. The result was the same, a glaring 59-0 Chicago victory. Chicago took the title two days later with a 13-0 win over the Hammond Pros. When Milwaukee's varsity squad was discovered, league president Joe Carr fined and exiled Badgers owner Ambrose McGurk. The franchise was sold off, played an unimpressive 2-7 season, and eventually disbanded.

# OORANG INDIANS

*Seasons Played in the NFL* 1922–1923

*Lifetime Record* 4-16

*Best Season* 1922, eleventh place (3-6)

The Oorang Indians were a traveling dog show . . . literally. Indians owner Walter Lingo was a breeder who saw the team as the best advertising return on investment he could get for his kennel. Lingo was also fascinated with Native American culture, and put together an "All-Indian" team led by Jim Thorpe to take to the road (the team only had one home game over two seasons) and showcase his dogs. Each game included an elaborate halftime show where the dogs did tricks for the crowds as Indian performers danced and demonstrated various native skills, including tomahawk throwing and lassoing. The main event (outside of the game) featured one of the Oorang players wrestling a bear. As for the non-circus portion of the team's existence, an almost-respectable 1922 season included a victory in their only home game, as well as two more on the road, one against a strong Buffalo team. Attendance eventually dropped, and the team ended its run the following year.

# RACINE LEGION/
# RACINE TORNADOES

### Seasons Played in the NFL
1922–1924, 1926

### Lifetime Record 15-15-6

### Best Season 1922, sixth place (6-4-1)

The Racine Legion took their name as a semi-pro team from an American Legion sponsorship. It was an appropriate banner to play under, as an earlier incarnation of the team had called itself the Battery C, on account of the number of players to join that particular unit of Wisconsin's Reserve Artillery prior to World War I. The Legion took to the NFL field in 1922 and played well, finishing the season at 6-4-1 behind Hank Gillo, the league's leading scorer. While the team finished at or above .500 for the next two seasons, it failed to generate enough fan interest to stay afloat. They were inactive for a year but came back as the Tornadoes in 1926, as the league looked to keep as much talent away from the would-be rival AFL. A 1-4 finish marked the end of NFL football in Racine.

# TOLEDO MAROONS/
# KENOSHA MAROONS

*Seasons Played in the NFL* 1922–1924

*Lifetime Record* 8-9-5

*Best Season* 1922, fourth place (5-2-2)

In the years leading up to World War I, Ohio was a hotbed for professional football, with many of the early APFA/NFL teams emerging from the Buckeye State. Toledo's entrant was no stranger to the likes of the Columbus Panhandles and Dayton Triangles, and officially joined the league as the Maroons in 1922. They were among the better teams in the league in their inaugural season but could not maintain their success and quickly faded away. They played their final season out of Kenosha, Wisconsin, and finished a disappointing 0-4-1 before disbanding.

# DULUTH KELLEYS/DULUTH ESKIMOS/ORANGE TORNADOES/ NEWARK TORNADOES

*Seasons Played in the NFL*
1923–1927, 1929–1930

*Lifetime Record* 20-34-8

*Best Season* 1924, fourth place (5-1-0)

What may have been most interesting about the Duluth Kelleys was their original ownership structure, shared between the players on the field. The arrangement didn't last long, as the team was having more success on the field during their early seasons than they were in their account ledgers. After an 0-3 1925 campaign, the team brought on a legitimate draw in All-American Stamford fullback Ernie Nevers, renamed themselves the Eskimos, and went on a road trip that would have made Red Grange proud—29 games in under four months. The signing led to profits and wins, but neither lasted, and a year later the Eskimos were done in Duluth. The franchise was inactive for a year, sold, and moved to Orange, New Jersey, where they became the Orange Tornadoes. A year later they moved again, and as the Newark Tornadoes they went 1-10-1 before finally pulling the plug.

# CLEVELAND INDIANS/ CLEVELAND BULLDOGS

*Seasons Played in the NFL* 1923–1925, 1927

*Lifetime Record* 23-14-6

*Championship Season* 1924 (7-1-1)

The Tribe's history is tangled with that of the Canton Bulldogs. As their inaugural season drew to a close, the Indians had a shot at the title with one game left to play against contending Canton. The collision between the two teams may have left Cleveland flat on the field, as Canton trounced them 46-0, but if you can't beat them, buy them. Cleveland owner Sam Deutsch bought the financially struggling Canton club and merged the teams, creating the Cleveland Bulldogs. A contested title year followed, with Cleveland needing a league ruling in its favor to be awarded the championship over Chicago—Cleveland had the better winning percentage at the agreed-upon end of the season, but the Bears had won a head-to-head challenge a week later. The decision went in Cleveland's favor, and title in hand, Deutsch sold the Bulldogs back to Canton while maintaining his own Cleveland Bulldogs squad. The unmerged Bulldogs were both mediocre after the parting, and Cleveland folded a year later. A Bulldogs team resurfaced in Cleveland in 1927 as part of the NFL's league-wide defense against AFL incursion and folded again at the end of the season. Some sources list the records of the 1927 Bulldogs on its own, others include it with its predecessor, and it also gets mixed up with both the 1926 Kansas City Cowboys and the expansion 1928 Detroit Wolverines (many of the players and player/coach Roy Andrews left the former to join the Bulldogs, and then joined the latter after the Bulldogs folded).

# ST. LOUIS ALL-STARS

*Season Played in the NFL* 1923

*Lifetime Record* 1-4-2

*Season Finish* fourteenth place

The All-Stars were a true expansion franchise, assembled for size and strong on defense. Their single campaign in the NFL limited all but one opponent to 7 points or less. Unfortunately, there was no offense to complement their defensive might, and they themselves were held scoreless in all but one game.

# FRANKFORD YELLOW JACKETS

*Seasons Played in the NFL* 1924–1931

*Lifetime Record* 69-45-15

*Championship Season* 1926 (14-1-2)

The Yellow Jackets joined the NFL in 1924 and played for eight seasons. Frankford had several winning years, including a third-place finish in their inaugural campaign and a 14-1-2 record in 1926 that gave them the league title. The team folded in 1931 after an abysmal 13-point performance. All of 1931 yielded one victory, six losses, and a tie.

# KANSAS CITY BLUES/
# KANSAS CITY COWBOYS

*Seasons Played in the NFL* 1924–1926

*Lifetime Record* 12-15-1

*Best Season* 1926, fourth place (8-3)

Kansas City's largest obstacle in maintaining its early NFL franchise was location. The Blues entered the league in 1924 but had great difficulty in scheduling games against teams that didn't want to make the trip to play them. They changed their name to the Cowboys in 1925, and went on a two-year road trip that only saw them come home for the final two games of 1926. The 1926 season most likely would not have happened were it not for the threat of the AFL, but it did produce winning Kansas City football before the team folded. Many of the players and player/coach Roy Andrews moved on to Cleveland to join the resurrected Bulldogs at the end of the year.

# NEW YORK GIANTS

*Founded* 1925

## Ring of Honor

Tim Mara, Wellington Mara, Jack Mara, Bob Tisch, George Young, Steve Owen, Jim Lee Howell, Bill Parcells, Frank Gifford, Harry Carson, Lawrence Taylor, Phil Simms, Michael Strahan, George Martin, Sam Huff, Y. A. Tittle, Jessie Armstead, Armani Toomer, Tiki Barber, Ken Strong, Pete Gogolak, Andy Robustelli, Tuffy Leemans, Al Blozis, Mel Hein, Roosevelt Brown, Emien Tunnell, Charlie Conerly, Dick Lynck, Joe Morrison

## Retired Numbers

1—Ray Flaherty; 4—Tuffy Leemans; 7—Mel Hein; 11—Phil Simms; 14—Y. A. Tittle; 16—Frank Gifford; 32—Al Blozis; 40—Joe Morrison; 42—Charlie Conerly; 50—Ken Strong; 56—Lawrence Taylor

## Division/Conference Championships

18: 1933, 1934, 1935, 1938, 1939, 1941, 1944, 1946, 1956, 1958, 1959, 1961, 1962, 1963, 1986, 1990, 2000, 2007

## NFL Championships/Super Bowl Victories

7: 1927, 1934, 1938, 1956, Super Bowl XXI (1986), Super Bowl XXV (1990), Super Bowl XLII (2007)

The New York Football Giants were purchased for $500 by bookmaker Tim Mara and later handed off to his two sons, Jack and Wellington. The G-Men were a postseason fixture in the first half of their existence, making regular playoff appearances at the Polo Grounds and later Yankee Stadium through 1963. During this stretch they won several titles and stood on the losing side of the 1958 Championship game against the Baltimore Colts—considered and argued by many as the greatest game ever played.

In the years that followed, the team fell into disarray, with only two winning seasons over a fourteen-year stretch that saw the team also call both Shea Stadium and the Yale Bowl home. Things finally settled down after the team moved to Giants Stadium, when Commissioner Pete Rozelle placed George Young in charge as general manager. Young put together a strong team through solid drafting, and following the promotion of defensive coordinator Bill Parcells to head coach, once again the franchise had a regular place in the playoffs. Big Blue took home their first Super Bowl trophy at the conclusion of the 1986 season and another one four years later. They would return to the Super Bowl in 2000 and again in 2007, where quarterback Eli Manning found David Tyree to keep a late drive going and Plaxico Burress to take the lead and upset the unbeaten Patriots.

# PROVIDENCE STEAM ROLLER

*Seasons Played in the NFL* 1925–1931

*Lifetime Record* 41-31-11

*Championship Season* 1928 (8-1-2)

The Steam Roller were a formidable squad, as an independent club in the early 1920s (named as they were because of how they handled lesser opponents) and for several good seasons in the NFL. The highlight of their NFL existence came in 1928 when player/coach Jimmy Conzelman led them to their first and only NFL championship season. As the Great Depression became a reality for the American public in the years that followed, attendance suffered and the Steam Roller ended its NFL run after the 1931 season.

# POTTSVILLE MAROONS/
# BOSTON BULLDOGS

*Seasons Played in the NFL* 1925–1929

*Lifetime Record* 31-24-2

*Best Season* 1925, second place (10-2)

The Maroons' welcome to the NFL was a controversial one. Their 1925 championship run against the Chicago Cardinals is introduced elsewhere (see Milwaukee Badgers, page 47), but there was an additional twist to their lost title. From the owners' perspective, one of the primary functions of the NFL as an officiating body was to protect territorial rights, especially in regard to home attendance. The week-to-week gate revenue was what kept many of the teams afloat, and part of the scheduling process was to ensure that teams faced no other league competition to their anticipated Sunday crowds. After beating Chicago in a late-season head-on match, the Maroons were poised to take the title were it not for two factors. First, as previously discussed, Chicago racked up two easy wins in a week's time to overtake them in the standings. Perhaps the scandal over the Cardinals playing against high school players would have swayed the league decision, but Pottsville had its own violations to contend with. The Chicago match had failed to be a big enough draw and Pottsville had agreed to play Notre Dame in Philadelphia's Shibe Park the following week. The problem was that an NFL game at Shibe Park would infringe upon the Frankford Yellow Jackets, who also had a home game in the

Philadelphia area that weekend. Pottsville needed the gate, so they played the game anyway and were not only fined for doing so but got kicked out of the league as well. The eviction didn't last, as the team was readmitted the following season as part of the anti-AFL expansion. Another respectable season followed, but it was the last year of note. The team declined and was eventually sold and moved to Boston, where they finished out their last year before folding as the Boston Bulldogs.

# DETROIT PANTHERS

*Seasons Played in the NFL* 1925–1926

*Lifetime Record* 12-8-4

*Best Season* 1925, third place (8-2-2)

Detroit's second entry into the league (but the first to actually play under the NFL banner) played good defensive football but still suffered the same fate as their predecessors. Player/coach Jimmy Conzelman had the 1925 team within reach of the title before falling to third. The 1926 team stumbled out of the gate before going on a nice run, but the team would not make it to the 1927 season to find out whether they could build on that momentum.

# BROOKLYN LIONS/BROOKLYN HORSE LIONS/NEW YORK YANKEES/ STATEN ISLAND STAPLETONS

*Seasons Played in the NFL* 1926–1932

*Lifetime Record* 28-46-11

*Championships* 1922–1923

While many of the late-1920s teams owe a portion of their NFL existence to the AFL, no franchise has its history so intertwined with the competing league than Brooklyn's. The AFL's marquee team was clearly Grange's Yankees, but the league had established a good potential draw in Brooklyn with the Horsemen, led by Harry Stuhldreher of Notre Dame "Four Horsemen" fame. The Lions were created to compete with the Horsemen, but as the AFL faltered, the two teams attempted a merge before the end of the 1926 season, and the Brooklyn Horse Lions were born. Unfortunately, the franchise was indebted to New York Giants owner Tim Mara, and Mara collected at the end of the season, taking control of the neighboring club. With the AFL no longer in operation, having Red Grange as a draw to NFL crowds was palatable to everyone, so Mara leant the Brooklyn franchise to Grange's Yankees and allowed them to be called the New York Yankees, provided they played most of their games on the road. Grange got hurt, and the team never recovered. Two years later Mara sold the team outright to a Staten Island group, where they played out their final seasons as the Staten Island Stapletons.

# NEW YORK YANKEES[9]

*Season Played in the AFL* 1926

*Lifetime Record* 10-5

*Season Finish* second place

The New York Yankees of the AFL are discussed elsewhere in this book, both in their origins (see Red Grange: The Galloping Ghost, page 20) and in their post-AFL fate (see the Brooklyn Lions, page 61). Their lone AFL season was a box office success. An AFL matchup at Yankee Stadium between the Yankees and eventual league champion Philadelphia Quakers drew 22,000, while later that season the Giants and eventual NFL champion Frankford (whose home was just outside Philly) could only draw 10,000 to the same venue. The venture ultimately failed, with the majority of the teams disbanding before season's end. Grange's Yankees finished second before taking over the recently expanded Brooklyn franchise and joining the NFL the following season.

---

9 It was never the intention of this book to profile all of the AFL teams (nor the many teams that comprised the other competing leagues—XFL, anyone?). However, the Yankees' history is so intertwined with the NFL's that an entry separate from their link to the Brooklyn/Staten Island franchise seemed in order.

# LOS ANGELES BUCCANEERS

*Season Played in the NFL* 1926

*Lifetime Record* 6-3-1

*Season Finish* sixth place

The Los Angeles Buccaneers did not play in Los Angeles; they were an LA team in name only. It would be another twenty years before the NFL played California football, through the 49ers and the All-American Football Conference's (AAFC's) LA Dons. The Buccaneers, like so many of the brief-history teams that took to the NFL field in the late 1920s, did so only to overwhelm the AFL and ensure that there was as little talent as possible for the fledgling league. The Bucs did manage a strong defensive season, limiting opposing teams to 15 points or less, including four shutouts (one a scoreless tie) in their only season of play.

# HARTFORD BLUES

*Season Played in the NFL* 1926

*Lifetime Record* 3-7

*Season Finish* thirteenth place

At one point in their independent existence, the Blues employed each of Notre Dame's legendary Four Horsemen of the Apocalypse: Harry Stuhldreher, Jim Crowley, Don Miller, and Elmer Layden. Originally out of Waterbury, the team played strong semi-pro regional ball following its move to Hartford. When the NFL expanded in 1926, the Blues were a natural addition but were left out once the competition from the AFL was no longer a factor.

# DETROIT WOLVERINES

*Season Played in the NFL* 1928

*Lifetime Record* 7-2-1

*Season Finish* third place

Detroit's third effort at fielding a permanent team went the way of their first two. The Wolverines picked up the remnants of player/coach Roy Andrews' Cleveland team and ran with it, finishing in third place in their only season. Fortunately for Detroit, the Wolverines would be the last false-start in their search for a stable franchise.

# DETROIT LIONS

## *Portsmouth Spartans (1930–1933)*

### *Founded* 1930

### *Pride of the Lions*
Lem Barney, Jack Christiansen, Dutch Clark, Lou Creekmur,
Dick "Night Train" Lane, Yale Lary, Bobby Lane, Dick LeBeau,
Barry Sanders, Charlie Sanders, Joe Schmidt, Doak Walker,
Alex Wojciechowicz

### *Retired Numbers*
7—Dutch Clark; 20— Barry Sanders; 22—Bobby Lane;
37—Doak Walker; 56—Joe Schmidt; 85—Chuck Hughes

### *Division Championships*
5: 1935, 1952, 1953, 1954, 1957

### *NFL Championships*
4: 1935, 1952, 1953, 1957

Detroit's third effort at fielding an NFL team took hold as the Lions were purchased and moved from Portsmouth, Ohio, in 1934. Not only did Detroit have a team again, they had a good team. The original Lions were contending for the division title against defending champions Chicago when both clubs met on Thanksgiving in a game broadcasted coast to coast on the NBC Radio Network. The Bears won the game, but the Lions walked away with an American tradition—Thanksgiving NFL football. The Lions would go on to win their division the following year, as well as their first title, beating the New York Giants in the championship game.

# BROOKLYN DODGERS/
# BROOKLYN TIGERS

*Seasons Played in the NFL* 1930–1944

*Lifetime Record* 60-100-9

*Best Season Finish*
1940 (8-3), 1941 (7-4): second in NFL East

The Brooklyn Dodgers were the only expansion team from the NFL's first decade to survive into the divisional era that began in 1933 but not make it for the long haul. The Dodger franchise was technically linked to the Dayton Triangles, but much like the Browns and the Ravens of the modern game, both teams are historically treated as separate clubs. The club's best years were in the early 1940s, and after losing several players to military service, they began to decline. The Dodgers' final year in the NFL was played as the Brooklyn Tigers. They were then merged with the Boston Yanks in 1945 to consolidate resources to keep the league running during World War II. The following year the club's ownership moved the franchise over to the AAFC where they became the New York Yankees. The AAFC had its own Brooklyn Dodgers, who were eventually merged with the Yankees, who upon the demise of the AAFC rejoined the NFL by merging again with the Boston Yanks, now playing out of New York as the New York Bulldogs.

# WASHINGTON REDSKINS

## Boston Braves (1932); Boston Redskins (1933–1936)

### Founded 1932

### Ring of Fame

George Allen, Cliff Battles, Sammy Baugh, Gene Brito, Larry Brown,
Dave Butz, Gary Clark, Jack Kent Cooke, Bill Dudley, Wayne Curry,
Pat Fischer, Joe Gibbs, Darrell Green, Russ Grimm, Chris Hanburger,
Ken Harvey, Len Hauss, Phil Hochberg, Ken Houston, Sam Huff,
Joe Jacoby, Dick James, Sonny Jurgensen, Charlie Justice,
Billy Kilmer, Eddie LeBaron, Vince Lombardi, Dexter Manley,
Charles Mann, George Preston Marshall, Wayne Millner, Bobby
Mitchell, Brian Mitchell, Art Monk, Mark Moseley, Brig Owens,
Vince Promuto, John Riggins, Jerry Smith, Charley Taylor,
Sean Taylor, Joe Theismann, Lamar "Bubba" Tyer

### Retired Numbers 33—Sammy Baugh

### Conference Championships

11: 1936, 1937, 1940, 1942, 1943, 1945, 1972, 1982, 1983, 1987, 1991

### NFL Championships/Super Bowls

5: 1937; 1942; Super Bowl XVII (1982); Super Bowl XXII (1987);
Super Bowl XXVI (1991)

The Redskins originated in Boston, playing their inaugural season at Braves Field (home of National League baseball's Boston Braves, who eventually left town for Milwaukee before settling in Atlanta). A year later, when the team relocated to Fenway Park, they changed their name to the Redskins as a nod to the Red Sox. The 'Skins took an Eastern Division, but playing at Fenway didn't do anything for the team's attendance, so much so that they gave up the home field advantage and chose a neutral site for the championship game, losing to Green Bay at New York's Polo Grounds. The next season the team moved again, this time to Washington, D.C.

The Redskins' 75-year history playing out of D.C. is deep with tradition, kicking off with a stretch of playoff appearances that spanned from their arrival through World War II and included two league titles in six appearances. They were also on the wrong end of the most lopsided defeat in professional championship football history, losing 73-0 to the Chicago Bears in the 1940 title game. Competitively dormant through the postwar years, the team returned to prominence after the AFL/NFL merge, making 16 playoff appearances, resulting in five NFC titles and three Super Bowl victories. The team's resurgence is largely credited to head coach Joe Gibbs, whose decade-plus run (along with a twenty-first century comeback) made him the winningest coach in franchise history. It was also during Gibbs's reign that the team's fans bore witness to one of the more gruesome sights in the history of the sport, as Lawrence Taylor broke Redskins quarterback Joe Theismann's leg on national television during a Monday Night Football game in 1985. While the team finished out Gibbs's initial run strong, most Redskins fans feel as if the two decades that followed were the equivalent of that fateful sack replayed on an endless loop. Gibbs's return did produce playoff appearances in 2004 and 2007.

"Slingin Sammy" Baugh, who joined the Washington Redskins in 1937

Practice uniforms have certainly changed over the past century

# 1920–1932 APFA/NFL CHAMPIONS

**1920:** Akron Pros (8-0-3)

**1921:** Chicago Staleys (9-1-1)

**1922:** Canton Bulldogs (10-0-2)

**1923:** Canton Bulldogs (11-0-1)

**1924:** Cleveland Bulldogs (7-1-1)

**1925:** Chicago Cardinals (11-2-1)

**1926:** Frankford Yellow Jackets (14-1-2)

**1927:** New York Giants (11-1-1)

**1928:** Providence Steam Rollers (8-1-2)

**1929:** Green Bay Packers (12-0-1)

**1930:** Green Bay Packers (10-3-1)

**1931:** Green Bay Packers (12-2)

**1932:** Chicago Bears (7-1-6)

# 1933–1965

With the NFL East and NFL West, 1933 saw the beginning of divisional play in the NFL. The winners of each league would meet in an annual title game to decide the league champion. Ties within the division were settled with a one-game playoff, with the winner advancing to the final.

Franchises came and went in the years leading up to World War II, as did another challenger to the league—the second short-lived AFL. The most successful of these new teams to take the field were the Rams (then out of Cleveland), the Eagles, and the Steelers. During the war, several teams were forced to suspend operations, while others temporarily merged, bringing about the likes of the Steagles and the Card-Pitts (sometimes referred to as the "Carpets" on account of the rest of the league walking all over them).

---

### THE RECORDS
In his rookie season for the 1952 Los Angeles Rams,
Dick "Night Train" Lane set the since-unbroken record for
most interceptions in a season, at 14.

---

The 1950s not only saw the Pro Bowl become an annual contest but also brought three significant events that impacted the development of the professional game. The first was something of a gift. As the rules to football were still being tweaked over the years, college football began allowing for unlimited substitution of players. Platoon play with offensive and defensive units (as opposed to the early style in which most players stayed on the field for the entire game) made for a more energetic game, and the NFL quickly followed. When the NCAA reversed their decision, the NFL was all alone with the style of play that the growing football fan base preferred. Now when people talked about football, they talked about the NFL.

The 1950s also brought another significant change to the league—the merger with the All-America Football Conference (AAFC). Following World War II, the AAFC was formed and placed teams in New York, Brooklyn, Cleveland, Miami, Los Angeles, Buffalo, and San Francisco. The new league immediately competed with the NFL for talent—especially in Cleveland. Paul Brown of the Cleveland Browns recruited heavily from Ohio State, where he had won a national championship as a coach, and outsigned the senior league for the rights to Otto Graham, among others. The Browns dominated the league with a championship win each season, so much so that they may have smothered the potential for interest in the other young franchises before it could fully develop into loyal followings. The AAFC accepted a merger proposal, with Cleveland, San Francisco, and Baltimore (relocated from Miami) joining the NFL. The Dons out of Los Angeles were absorbed by the Rams, and the two New York teams picked apart the Yankees, with the rest of the AAFC players made available to the league through a disbursal draft.

# JIM BROWN

In the 1950s, the only thing that may have surpassed Jim Brown's skill in running the football may have been Jim Brown's skill at playing lacrosse. Fortunately for the NFL, the first-team All-American out of Syracuse University chose football. Brown was drafted by the Cleveland Browns in 1956 and was a star from the get-go, taking the field as a rookie and owning it for nine years, a stretch in which he never missed a game.

He was unanimously voted Rookie of the Year in 1957 and four times during his career was voted league Most Valuable Player (1957, 1958, 1963, and 1965). He is the only rusher in NFL history to average over 100 yards per game for a career.

The AAFC's Colts didn't last in the NFL, but following the demise of the Dallas Texans, Carroll Rosenbloom in Baltimore was assured that if he could sell enough season ticket pledges, a replacement franchise would be awarded to the city. Four weeks later, with 15,000 season tickets sold, the Baltimore Colts were reborn. These Colts would play a part in what is now regarded as one of the most pivotal moments in league history. As the age of television was upon the American population, the 1958 championship game became an event for the ages. Televised before a national audience estimated at more than 45 million, the nation tuned in to see Johnny Unitas and the Colts take on the New York Giants. The televised audience could have been bigger, but because the game was played in New York, blackout restrictions prevented it from being broadcast to the local audience (an eventual refinement of this rule would only call for a blackout if the stadium attendance was below an agreed-upon threshold). The game would feature twelve eventual hall-of-famers and became the only championship game to go into overtime. The Colts won, but so did the league, as the game's popularity was launched into a new stratosphere.

The 1958 championship game showed the country the potential of the NFL as a business. When the time to negotiate a television contract came, Giants owner Wellington Mara realized that the success of the smallest of teams would impact the success of the league as a whole, and successfully pushed for revenue sharing of the TV deal even though he occupied the country's major media market.

*We are inclined to think that if we watch a football game or a baseball game, we have taken part in it.*

**—John F. Kennedy**

# VINCE LOMBARDI

Vince Lombardi ran one of the most celebrated professional football programs in the history of the NFL, leading the Green Bay Packers to six championship appearances and five titles in eight years. Lombardi got his start at St. Cecilia High School, and coached at Fordham University and West Point before accepting a position as an assistant with the New York Giants. He made a name for himself in New York but still had difficulty moving on to the next level and was repeatedly rejected, sometimes without reply, in his efforts to land a major head coaching position. When Green Bay offered him the head coaching job, the club was in complete disarray, having finished the previous season 1-10-1. He accepted nonetheless, and as legend goes, Vince Lombardi declared to the team during his first address that he had "never been on a losing team ... and I do not intend to start now." Like a spell, it worked, and the Lombardi era was a winning one.

Following the game, Giants offensive coordinator Vince Lombardi was called on to take over the head coaching position in Green Bay. His historic run hit a bump in the road in 1963 when his running back and one-time MVP was suspended by new commissioner Pete Rozelle for gambling. Fully aware of the impact that gambling had had on baseball decades earlier, Rozelle knew he could not afford to squander the league's newfound momentum.

Following the 1958 championship, the potential of the game was also observed by business rivals. Texas billionaire Lamar Hunt, after failing in his bid to buy the Cardinals, put together a group to launch their own league. The AFL would battle the NFL over part of the next decade, jockeying for talent as well as for cities. As it was in the 1920s, the rival league prompted NFL expansion. After turning down a group looking to expand the NFL into Minnesota, the AFL swooped in and added them to their franchise roster, only to have the NFL reverse its decision and embrace the Vikings. Losing Minnesota from the AFL left the Los Angeles Chargers with no close rival, and an Oakland team was admitted into the new league as well. The Raiders joined the Titans out of New York, the Houston Oilers, the Buffalo Bills, the Boston Patriots, the Dallas Texans, and the Denver Broncos. The Dallas team would eventually relocate to Kansas as the Chiefs, the Titans would rename themselves the Jets, and the AFL would challenge the league long enough to warrant an eventual meeting between league champions as the merger drumbeat began to sound.

# PHILADELPHIA EAGLES

## *Philadelphia/Pittsburgh Steagles (1943)*

### Founded
1933

### Honor Roll
Chuck Bednark, Bert Bell, Harold Carmichael, Bill Hewitt,
Sonny Jurgensen, Wilbert Montgomery, Earle "Greasy" Neale,
Pete Pihos, Ollie Matson, Jim Ringo, Norm Van Brocklin,
Steve Van Buren, Alex Wojciechowicz, Bill Bergey,
Tommy McDonald, Tom Brookshier, Pete Retzlaff, Timmy Brown,
Jerry Sisemore, Stan Walters, Ron Jaworski, Bill Bradley,
Dick Vermeil, Jim Gallagher, Mike Quick, Jerome Brown,
Otho Davis, Reggie White, Al Wistert, Randall Cunningham,
Eric Allen, Jim Johnson

### Retired Numbers
15—Steve Van Buren; 40—Tom Brookshier; 44—Pete Retzlaff;
60—Chuck Bednarik; 70—Al Wistert; 92—Reggie White;
99—Jerome Brown

### Division/Conference Championships
7: 1947, 1948, 1949, 1969, 1980, 2001, 2004

### NFL Championships 3: 1948, 1949, 1969

The Eagles came into the NFL and mostly floundered through their early seasons, not really taking shape as a team until the 1940s. Following a brief merger with Pittsburgh to form the Steagles, Philly went on a successful run, taking home a pair of consecutive titles in 1948 and 1949.

For many, mention of the Eagles evokes stories of their fans. While some of them are true, the Eagles should be remembered for more than having fans who once booed Santa Claus. While it's true that old Saint Nick wasn't made to feel too welcome in Philly, in fairness to the City of Brotherly Love, it was December, the team had just won its second game of the season—which effectively knocked them out of the O. J. Simpson sweepstakes for the following year's draft—they had blown a 7-0 lead right before the first half expired, and the scheduled Santa Claus got stuck in the mud. A substitute Santa was pulled from the crowd and thrown out to the lions, where he was mercilessly booed and pelted with snow. While there was much frustration in Philadelphia during that 1968 season, a year later it would be forgotten, as the Eagles bounced back to win the NFL championship, their third and last.

# CLEVELAND INDIANS

*Season Played in the NFL* 1931

*Lifetime Record* 2-8-0

*Season Finish* eighth place

Another failed effort to launch a franchise in the city of Cleveland, this Tribe was owned and operated by the NFL in an "if you build it, they will come" move, with the "they" being investors. None came; the team finished poorly and folded.

# CINCINNATI REDS/
# ST. LOUIS GUNNERS

*Seasons Played in the NFL* 1933–1934

*Lifetime Record* 4-16

*Best Season* 1933, fourth place (3-6)

---

## THE RECORDS

In 1932 the NFL began keeping track of single-season touchdown statistics. The following year the anemic offense of the Cincinnati Reds scored three touchdowns, the current record for fewest touchdowns scored—although it is safe to assume that the 1922 and 1926 Hammond Pros could make an argument for the record, as the former scored zero points and the latter only three. The informal scheduling of the 1920s gives the non-glory to Cincinnati, who also had the fewest yards gained (1,150) and fewest passes completed (25).

---

Cincinnati came into the league with Philadelphia and Pittsburgh as part of a strategy to expand into every major city the NFL could reach. While the latter two franchises flourished, the Reds stumbled. Their 3-6 record in 1933 was nothing they could build off, as the 1934 team was 0-8 when ownership sold it to a group in St. Louis. Now the Gunners, the St. Louis-operated group finished out the last three games of the '34 season with a single win before folding the franchise.

# PITTSBURGH STEELERS

*Pittsburgh Pirates (1933–1939); Philadelphia/Pittsburgh Steagles (1943); Pittsburgh/Chicago Card-Pitt (1944)*

*Founded* 1933

*Retired Numbers* 70—Ernie Stautner

*Conference Championships*
8: 1974, 1975, 1978, 1979, 1995, 2005, 2008, 2010

*Super Bowl Victories*
6: 1974, 1975, 1978, 1979, 2005, 2008

---

### THE RECORDS

The Detroit Lions rushed for 426 yards against the Pittsburgh Pirates on November 4, 1934—the most yards gained on the ground in a single game.

---

Founded by Art Rooney, the Pirates struggled in their early years. After the team was rebranded the Steelers in 1940, they had their first winning season. The momentum was briefly interrupted by World War II, when, to maintain a team, the Steelers temporarily merged with the Eagles in 1943 and the Cardinals in 1944. The latter pairing was simply named Card-Pitt, but the team played so poorly that it was referred to by many as the "Carpet." Following the war, the team advanced to its first playoff appearance. In the 1960s the Steelers introduced the now-iconic logo that appears on their helmets, which is based on the Steelmark logo of the American Iron and Steel Institute.

Following the NFL/AFL merger, the Steelers accepted a transfer into the AFC. It proved to be a most prosperous move, as the 1970s saw the Steelers rise to elite status, with a dynasty team that took home four Super Bowl trophies over six years.

# ST. LOUIS RAMS

*Cleveland Rams (1937–1945);*
*Los Angeles Rams (1946–1994)*

## *Founded* 1937

## *Ring of Fame*
Bob Waterfield, Norm Van Brocklin, Eric Dickerson,
Elroy "Crazylegs" Hirsch, Tom Fears, Tom Mack, Merlin Olsen,
David "Deacon" Jones, Jackie Slater, Jack Snow, Jack Youngblood,
Dick Vermeil, Dan Reeves, Carrol Rosenbloom, Georgia Frontiere

## *Retired Numbers*
7—Bob Waterfield; 28—Marshall Faulk; 29—Eric Dickerson;
74—Merlin Olsen; 75—David "Deacon" Jones; 78—Jackie Slater;
80—Isaac Bruce; 85—Jack Youngblood

## *Division/Conference Championships*
8: 1945, 1949, 1950, 1951, 1955, 1979, 1999, 2001

## *NFL Championships/Super Bowl Victories*
3: 1945, 1951, Super Bowl XXXIV (1999)

## THE RECORDS

On November 19, 1950, in a game between the Los Angeles Rams and the New York Yanks, the Rams moved the ball for 636 total yards against the Yanks' 497. Their combined 1,133 yards-gained stands as the most ever in a single game.

The Rams began their existence in Cleveland, taking the name of a team from the second AFL experiment that finished second in that league the previous year but eventually folded. The NFL's Rams spent eight years in Cleveland (taking one year off during World War II) before making the move to Los Angeles. In 1946 the LA Rams signed Woody Strode and Kenny Washington out of UCLA. Together the two Bruin teammates were the first African-American players to play in the modern NFL. It has been suggested that their signing paved the way for Branch Rickey to sign their teammate (and Washington's roommate) Jackie Robinson to baseball's Brooklyn Dodgers the following year.

The LA team played competitive football in its first few seasons, especially after the demise of the AAFC eliminated the competition for local talent. Pete Rozelle came on as a publicist for the Rams and eventually was hired to take over as general manager—a position he maintained until Bert Bell passed away and Rozelle was elected as league commissioner. After the merge, the Rams were regular playoff participants through the late 1980s, when the team went into decline. In 1995 the team moved back across the country, returning football to St. Louis (which had recently lost the Cardinals) and rewarding their new fans with a Super Bowl championship three years later—the first franchise championship of the post-merge era.

# BOSTON YANKS/NEW YORK BULLDOGS/NEW YORK YANKS

*Seasons Played in the NFL* 1944–1951

*Lifetime Record* 23-62-6

*Best Season* 1950, third place (7-5)

---

### THE RECORDS

On September 28, 1951, the Los Angeles Rams gained 735 yards against the defense of the New York Yanks—the most ever gained by a team in a single game.

---

Yanks owner Ted Collins wanted a New York franchise, but the strong territorial rights held by the Giants pushed him into Boston. He kept the Yankee-inspired name, but not enough of it to field a winning team. After four losing seasons (one of which included a merger with the Brooklyn Tigers during World War II) he finally got permission to move the club into New York and did so as the New York Bulldogs. A year later he changed the name and the New York Yanks had their only winning season. The magic didn't last, as the 1951 team went 1-9-2 and folded in the offseason.

# BROOKLYN DODGERS/
# BROOKLYN–NEW YORK YANKEES

*Seasons Played in the AAFC* 1946–1949

*Lifetime Record* 16-36-2

*Best Season* 1950, third place (8-4)

The Dodgers were part of the AAFC and had a brief history of losing seasons before the AAFC folded. The one highlight of the Dodgers' existence was their merger with the AAFC's New York team, the Yankees (not to be confused with the NFL's Yanks), in 1949. The combined team went 8-4 and earned a playoff berth. The AAFC's roster had thinned out in its final year and used a pair of semifinal playoff rounds to determine who would advance to the championship game. The multiborough team played San Francisco and lost.

# MIAMI SEAHAWKS/
# BALTIMORE COLTS

*Season Played in the AAFC/NFL* 1946–1950

*Lifetime Record* 14-51-1

*Best Season*
1948, first place in AAFC East Division (7-7)

An AAFC charter team, the Seahawks were the first professional sports team to play for the state of Florida. Overrun with debt, the franchise was sold to a Baltimore group and reborn the Colts in 1947. The Colts had one decent season, making it to the 1948 divisional playoff before losing to the Bills, but their legacy is both their survival into the NFL for one season following the AAFC/NFL merger and the fan base they created that would get behind the modern Colts franchise (before having their hearts broken at its departure).

# BUFFALO BISONS/BUFFALO BILLS

*Seasons Played in the AAFC* 1946–1949

*Lifetime Record* 23-36-5

*Best Season* 1948, division champion (7-7)

The Bills came into the AAFC as the Bisons, a throwback to the early NFL team. Buffalo produced a very competitive AAFC entry, making it to the AAFC Championship game in 1948 and returning to the playoffs in its final season. Many believed that the Bills should have been included with the Browns, 49ers, and Colts in the AAFC/NFL merger. League politics were said to be a factor in keeping the Buffalo franchise out of the NFL, and its ownership took a small stake and a handful of players to the Browns, leaving the rest to be distributed in the dispersal draft.

# LOS ANGELES DONS

### Seasons Played in the AAFC
1946–1949

### Lifetime Record
25-27-2

### Best Season
1946, third place (7-5-2)

The Dons had a mediocre run in the AAFC, with only one winning season and no playoff appearances. They were kept out of the merger directly but to some degree were absorbed by the Rams at the conclusion of the 1949 season.

# NEW YORK YANKEES

### Seasons Played in the AAFC
1946–1949

### Lifetime Record
35-17-2

### Best Season
1946 (10-3-1)–1947 (11-2-1), first place AAFC Eastern Division

The Yankees challenged the Browns for supremacy in the AAFC in the first two years of the league's existence, losing the championship game both times. The team eventually merged with the Brooklyn franchise, and following the fall of the league had most of its players disbursed to the NFL's Giants and Yanks.

# CLEVELAND BROWNS

*Founded* 1946

*Ring of Honor*

Jim Brown, Paul Brown, Joe DeLamielleure, Len Ford, Frank Gatski,
Otto Graham, Lou Groza, Gene Hickerson, Leroy Kelly,
Dante Lavelli, Mike McCormack, Bobby Mitchell, Marion Motley,
Ozzie Newsome, Paul Warfield, Bill Willis

*Retired Numbers*

14—Otto Graham; 32—Jim Brown; 45—Ernie Davis;
46—Don Fleming; 76—Lou Groza

*Division/Conference Championships*

13: 1946, 1947, 1948, 1949, 1950, 1951, 1952, 1953, 1954,
1955, 1957, 1964, 1965

*AAFC/NFL Championships*

8: 1946 (AAFC), 1947 (AAFC), 1948 (AAFC), 1949 (AAFC),
1950, 1954, 1955, 1964

---

### THE RECORDS

Jim Brown was the league leader in rushing eight times (1957–1961,
1963–1965) and the league leader in rushing touchdowns for five
(1957–1959, 1963, 1965). No other player has dominated
his peers for as many seasons.

---

The Browns were the powerhouse of the AAFC. At the helm was former Ohio State national championship-winning coach Paul Brown, who begrudgingly agreed to the fans' vote of sharing his name with the team's after it was suggested that the team was actually being named for Joe Louis—the "Brown Bomber." Brown made waves by waging a signing war with the NFL, picking up Otto Graham and others before they could join the senior league. After the AAFC merged with the NFL, Brown's Browns proved they belonged by winning the league championship in their first season, and making it to the title game in each of the next five. They made it back to the title game in 1957 with former Syracuse University star running back Jim Brown at the beginning of his dominant NFL career, but only won one title during Brown's tenure, this after Coach Brown had been shockingly fired by owner Art Modell. Thirty years later Modell would devastate the Cleveland faithful when he moved the team to Baltimore in 1995 and renamed them the Ravens. Fortunately, the city retained the franchise's history, and the expansion Browns resumed the Cleveland football legacy in 1999, returning to the playoffs in 2002.

# CHICAGO ROCKETS/
# CHICAGO HORNETS

## Seasons Played in the AAFC
1946–1949

## Lifetime Record 11-40-3

## Best Season
1946, fourth place AAFC West (5-6-3)

The Rockets tried to make a place for themselves in a crowded market and failed. The AAFC team could not hold its own against the Bears and the Cardinals, especially playing losing football. The team changed its name to the Hornets in 1949 and closed up shop after the AAFC/ NFL merger.

# DALLAS TEXANS

*Season Played in the NFL* 1952

*Lifetime Record* 1-11

*Season Finish* sixth place

In their first seven games, the expansion Dallas Texans scored more than 100 points. Unfortunately, they were outscored by 140. Ownership had to forfeit the team back to the league due to financial difficulties, and the team finished the season with a lone win on Thanksgiving Day before folding at the end of the season.

# SAN FRANCISCO 49ERS

## *Founded* 1946

## *49ers Hall of Fame*

Edward DeBartolo Jr., Leo Nomellini, Joe Perry, Hugh McElhenny,
Y. A. Tittle, John Henry Johnson, Bob St. Clair, Bill Walsh,
Jimmy Johnson, Joe Montana, Ronnie Lott, Dave Wilcox,
Steve Young, Fred Dean, Charlie Kruger, John Brodie, Jerry Rice,
Tony Morabito, Vic Morabito, Roger Craig, R. C. Owens

## *Retired Numbers*

8—Steve Young; 12—John Brodie; 16—Joe Montana; 34—Joe Perry;
37—Jimmy Johnson; 39—Hugh McElhenny; 42—Ronnie Lott;
70—Charlie Krueger; 73—Leo Normellini; 79—Bob St. Clair;
80—Jerry Rice;  87—Dwight Clark

## Division/Conference Championships
6: 1949, 1981, 1984, 1988, 1989, 1994

## Super Bowl Victories
5: Super Bowl XVI (1981), Super Bowl XIX (1984),
Super Bowl XXIII (1988), Super Bowl XXIV (1989),
Super Bowl XXIX (1994)

The 49ers were a charter AAFC team that survived the merger with the NFL and after a slow start ultimately thrived in their new home. Under head coach Bill Walsh and a group of all-time players including Jerry Rice, Joe Montana, Ronnie Lott, and Roger Craig, the 'Niners won three Super Bowls. After Walsh left, his replacement, Coach George Seifert, would see the team win two more, putting San Francisco at 5-1 in championship games (including the 1949 AAFC title match against Cleveland) and 5-0 in the Super Bowl.

# If you can believe it, the mind can achieve it.

**—Ronnie Lott**

# INDIANAPOLIS COLTS

## Baltimore Colts (1953–1983)

### Founded
1953

### Ring of Honor
Jim Harbaugh, Chris Hinton, Bill Brooks, Tony Dungy, Robert Isray,
Ted Marchibroda, 12th Man (the fans)

### Retired Numbers
19—Johnny Unitas; 22—Buddy Young; 24—Lenny Moore;
70—Art Donovan; 77—Jim Parker; 82—Raymond Berry;
89—Gino Marchetti

### Division/Conference Championships
8: 1958, 1959, 1964, 1965, 1968, 1970, 2006, 2009

### NFL Championships/Super Bowl Victories
4: 1958, 1959, Super Bowl IV (1970), Super Bowl XLI (2006)

## THE RECORDS

On December 9, 1956, Johnny Unitas, a mostly unknown player who had started the season on the Baltimore Colts' bench, threw a 3-yard touchdown pass to receiver Jim Mutscheller in a 31-7 loss to the Los Angeles Rams. Four years and two days later Unitas would face the Rams again. In between, the Colts became his team and he became an icon, completing 10,645 passing yards and 102 TD passes in a since-unapproachable record streak of 47 consecutive games with at least one touchdown pass.

Carroll Rosenbloom gathered enough support from the AAFC's remaining Colts fans to bring football back to Baltimore. In thirty years of play, the Baltimore Colts had a lasting impact on the league, having hosted Johnny Unitas's streak, played and won "The Greatest Game," legitimized the AFL merge by losing to the Jets and Joe Namath's guarantee in the first championship game called the "Super Bowl" (Super Bowls I and II were retroactively retitled), and also having the footnote of being traded by ownership for another team (the Los Angeles Rams). The story of the Colts in Baltimore is one that included a shocking twist for its supporters, as the team was literally packed up in the middle of the night and moved to Indianapolis by ownership before alerting the public that such a move was going to happen.

The Indianapolis version of the Colts suffered the karma of their move until the turn of the century, when they selected Archie Manning's son Peyton with the first overall pick in the 1999 draft. A perennial playoff contender, Manning's Colts won the Super Bowl in 2006.

# BUFFALO BILLS

*Founded* 1960

*Retired Numbers*
12—Jim Kelly

*Division/Conference Championships*
6: 1964, 1965, 1990, 1991, 1992, 1993

*AFL Championships* 2: 1964, 1965

---

### THE RECORDS

O. J. Simpson rushed for 200 yards or more in a game six times during his career, twice over two consecutive games (against the Patriots and the Jets in 1973, the second time against the Lions and the Dolphins in 1976); no other player has rushed for as many 200+ yard games, and only Earl Campbell (1980) and Ricky Williams (2002) have hit the same mark on consecutive games.

When the AAFC's Bills weren't included in the merger that brought the Colts, Browns, and 49ers to the NFL, some were confused. That team had played well and established a strong regional following. Their absence from the merger roster presented a clear void that the AFL was able to exploit by including Buffalo among its charter franchises. The Bills did well in the old AFL, winning the last two league titles before the merge.

Buffalo returned to prominence in the early 1990s, as the only team to win four consecutive conference titles. Unfortunately, none of their Super Bowl appearances ended well, with losses to the Cowboys and Redskins and a tragic upset from the Giants, in which Scott Norwood's potential game-winning field goal went wide right as the clock expired.

# DALLAS COWBOYS

*Founded* 1960

*Ring of Honor*

Bob Lilly, Don Meredith, Don Perkins, Chuck Howley, Mel Renfro,
Roger Staubach, Lee Roy Jordan, Tom Landry, Tony Dorsett,
Randy White, Bob Hayes, Tex Schramm, Cliff Harris,
Rayfield Wright, Troy Aikman, Michael Irvin, Emmitt Smith,
Drew Pearson, Charles Haley, Larry Allen

*Division/Conference Championships*

8: 1970, 1971, 1975, 1977, 1978, 1992, 1993, 1995

*Super Bowl Victories*

5: Super Bowl VI (1971), Super Bowl XII (1977),
Super Bowl XXVII (1992), Super Bowl XXVIII (1993),
Super Bowl XXX (1995)

When the AFL announced it was adding a team in Dallas to its charter class, it came as no surprise that the NFL approved its own Dallas franchise to compete. While the Cowboys status as "America's team" may be questioned, they were clearly Texas's team, sending the Texans packing to Kansas City, where they became the Chiefs. For almost thirty years, Tom Landry ruled the Dallas sidelines. Forever remembered for his suit and hat, Landry led the Cowboys to five NFC championships and two titles.

When Landry stepped down in 1988, Jimmy Johnson became the second coach in Cowboys history and led the team to two more titles in the early 1990s. Today they are a regular player in the NFL's annual Thanksgiving Day games and rank first in value among sports franchises at an estimated $1.65 billion.

# KANSAS CITY CHIEFS

*Dallas Texans (1960–1962)*

*Founded* 1960

*Ring of Honor*

Lamar Hunt, Mack Lee Hill, Jerry Mays, Fred Arbanas,
Johnny Robinson, Chris Burford, E. J. Holub, Jim Tyrer, Mike
Garrett, Len Dawson, Bobby Bell, Buck Buchanan, Otis Taylor, Ed
Budde, Willie Lanier, Emmitt Thomas, Hank Stram, Jerrel Wilson,
Ed Podolak, Jim Lynch, Abner Haynes, Jan Stenerud,
Sherrill Headrick, Jack Rudnay, Curtis McClinton, Deron Cherry,
Dave Hill, Art Still, Lloyd Burruss, Christian Okoye, Derrick Thomas,
John Alt, Gary Spani, Joe Delaney, Jack Steadman, Neil Smith,
Albert Lewis, Curley Culp, Nick Lowery, Marty Schottenheimer

*Retired Numbers*

3—Jan Stenerud; 16—Len Dawson; 18—Emmitt Thomas;
28—Abner Haynes; 33—Stone Johnson; 36—Mack Lee Hill;
63—Willie Lanier; 78—Bobby Bell; 86—Buck Buchanan

*Division/Conference Championships*

3: 1962, 1966, 1969

*AFL Championships/Super Bowl Victories*

2: 1962, Super Bowl IV (1969)

AFL founder Lamar Hunt relocated his team out of Texas and into Kansas City shortly after they began operation, but not before winning an AFL title in 1962. After beating Minnesota in Super Bowl IV, the Chiefs have been shut out of the championship game for more than forty years, with only a run of early round playoff exits in the 1990s and an appearance in the 1993 conference championship to show for their efforts.

---

### THE RECORDS

On November 16, 1964, Kansas City quarterback Len Dawson fumbled the ball seven times in a game against San Diego—the most ever by a player in a single game. Dawson's very bad day does not overshadow his six consecutive seasons leading the league in completions (1964–1969) and four times in touchdowns, also records (the latter shared with Johnny Unitas, Steve Young, and Brett Favre).

---

# BOBBY BELL

Bobby Bell was sought after by both the AFL's Chiefs and the NFL's Vikings—a big prize in the signing war between the rival leagues, and understandably so. The defensive end was a two-time All-American out of the University of Minnesota and was a member of the 1960 National Championship team. Bell ultimately ended up with Kansas City, where he excelled under coach Hank Stram and his "stack defense." His superb athleticism led Stram to say that "He could play all 22 positions on the field, and play them well."

Bell played on two AFL championship teams as well as Kansas City's only Super Bowl team. In the lead-up to the latter, he made a key goal line stop against the Jets during the divisional playoffs, forcing New York to kick a field goal in a game that Kansas City won 13-6. He finished his career with nine career touchdowns, six of them off interceptions (of which he had 26).

# DENVER BRONCOS

*Founded* 1960

*Ring of Fame* Austin "Goose" Gonsoulin, Rich Jackson, Floyd Little, Lionel Taylor, Gerald H. Phipps, Charley Johnson, Paul Smith, Frank Tripucka, Billy Thompson, Craig Morton, Haven Moses, Jim Turner, Randy Gradishar, Tom Jackson, Louis Wright, John Elway, Karl Mecklenburg, Dennis Smith, Gary Zimmerman, Steve Atwater, Terrell Davis, Shannon Sharpe

*Retired Numbers*
7—John Elway; 18—Frank Tripucka; 44—Floyd Little

*Conference Championships* 6: 1977, 1986, 1987, 1989, 1997, 1998

*Super Bowls*
2: Super Bowl XXXII (1997), Super Bowl XXXIII (1998)

The history of the Denver Broncos may include mention of their AFL roots and AFC title in 1978, where they lost to the Cowboys in Super Bowl XIII, but it is really the John Elway story. John Elway was the poster child for the "quarterback who couldn't win the big game," having lost three Super Bowls in the 1980s despite engineering some magnificent late-game drives to get his team there. Paired with running back Terrell Davis, Elway's team finally made it in 1997, and then did it again in 1998 for good measure.

# NEW ENGLAND PATRIOTS

## *Boston Patriots (1960–1970)*

*Founded* 1960

### New England Patriots Hall of Fame
John Hannah, Nick Buoniconti, Gino Cappelletti, Bob Dee,
Jim Lee Hunt, Steve Nelson, Babe Parilli, Mike Haynes,
Steve Grogan, Billy Sullivan

### Retired Numbers
20—Gino Cappelletti; 40—Mike Haynes; 57—Steve Nelson;
73—John Hannah; 78—Bruce Armstrong; 79—Jim Lee Hunt;
89—Bob Dee

### Division/Conference Championships
7: 1963, 1985, 1996, 2001, 2003, 2004, 2007

---

### THE RECORDS
Tom Brady's 50 touchdown passes in 2007 are the most completed by
a player in a single season. On the receiving end, Randy Moss caught
23 of them, also the most ever by a player in a single season.

---

### Super Bowl Victories
3: Super Bowl XXXVI (2001), Super Bowl XXXVIII (2003),
Super Bowl XXXIX (2004)

The NFL had not had much success in Boston, with the Redskins leaving for Chicago and the Yanks moving to New York, so the AFL stepped in with the Patriots. The Boston team lost the 1963 AFL championship game to the Chargers and did not have much success beyond that in their early years. The team moved their stadium into the suburbs and rechristened themselves the New England Patriots after the AFL/NFL merger.

The Pats were victims of the monstrous 1985 Chicago Bears, losing 46-10 in Super Bowl XX, and did not fully emerge until the mid-1990s. With Bill Parcells' coaching and Drew Bledsoe at quarterback, the team began making regular playoff appearances, including a conference championship and a loss to the Packers in Super Bowl XXXI. After Parcells' departure to the Jets, the team was briefly helmed by Pete Carroll before bringing on Bill Belichick (who turned down Parcells' vacated Jets coaching position to return to New England). The Pats officially turned the corner with Tom Brady at quarterback, putting together a dynasty team that brought home three Super Bowl trophies over the next four years. Following a scandal in which the team was accused of videotaping its opponents against league rules, they seemed to find a new gear and tore through the NFL during the 2007 season, becoming the first team since the 1972 Miami Dolphins to finish the regular season undefeated—and did so with two extra games on the schedule. Unlike those Dolphins, the Pats couldn't seal the deal, as David Tyree, the unlikeliest of receivers, caught what would be the last pass of his NFL career in Super Bowl XLII to preserve a fourth-quarter drive that would ultimately yield a game-winning touchdown for the New York Giants, denying the Pats their perfect season.

# NEW YORK JETS

## *New York Titans (1960–1962)*

*Founded* 1960

*Ring of Honor*
Joe Namath, Curtis Martin, Joe Klecko, Larry Grantham,
Freeman McNeil

*Retired Numbers*
12—Joe Namath; 13—Don Maynard; 73—Joe Klecko

*Conference Championships* 1: 1968

*Super Bowl Victories* 1: Super Bowl III (1968)

---

### THE RECORDS

The longest recorded punt in professional football history
was 98 yards, by Steve O'Neal of the New York Jets on
September 21, 1969, against the Denver Broncos.

---

*Titans are bigger and stronger than Giants* was the thought behind the naming of the franchise meant to represent the AFL in its new league. Playing out of the Polo Grounds (that at one time had housed the baseball Giants, football Giants, Yankees, and Mets), the Titans had financial difficulties, and owner Harry Wismer had to sell the team. New ownership came in, and with it a new name, the Jets, and eventually a new home, the recently built Shea Stadium. After hiring coach Weeb Ewbank away from Baltimore, the Jets were almost ready to compete. After drafting quarterback Joe Namath, who had won a national championship for Bear Bryant at the University of Alabama, the Jets were ready to shock the world.

Three years later, they got their chance, after advancing to the newly christened Super Bowl to take on the NFL-champion Baltimore Colts. The AFL and NFL had a merger agreement, and as the actual union drew closer there were still many who doubted that the AFL teams belonged on the same field as their NFL rivals. Namath had the bravado to suggest otherwise, declaring, "We're gonna win the game, I guarantee it." They did, and while many questions surround that game (Was it fixed? Why did Namath get the MVP for such a mediocre outing?), it cemented the merger in the minds of many.

Today's Jets have flirted with the playoffs sparingly, turning up the heat more often in recent years. Their furthest advancement since Joe Namath's guarantee has been four appearances in the AFC title game—one in the 1980s, one in the 1990s, and back-to-back appearances to close out the first decade of the twenty-first century.

# OAKLAND RAIDERS

### *Los Angeles Raiders (1982–1994)*

*Founded* 1960

*Division/Conference Championships*
5: 1967, 1976, 1980, 1983, 2002

*Super Bowl Victories*
3: Super Bowl XI (1976), Super Bowl XV (1980),
Super Bowl XVIII (1983)

---

## THE RECORDS
Ted Hendricks (Colts, Packers, Raiders) and Doug English (Lions)
both hold the record for most safeties in a career, with four.

---

Filling the scheduling void created by the loss of the Minnesota Vikings, the AFL's Oakland Raiders owe much to their neighbors to the south, the San Diego (formerly Los Angeles) Chargers. The Chargers' ownership saw the open slot as an opportunity to give them a natural rival on the West Coast and threatened the league that it would leave unless another California team was added. The city was awarded the franchise, briefly called the Oakland Señors before ever taking the field, and soon backed it with investors. Al Davis was soon hired to take over as coach and general manager, but he left the team after being named president of the AFL four years later. Following the merger, Davis was out of power and returned to the Raiders as a part owner. Some suggest this motivated his many legal battles with the league, prompting the team's relocation to and from Los Angeles. Davis soon took over operational control and was there to shake the hand of his rival, Commissioner Pete Rozelle, while accepting the Lombardi trophy after his "Just Win, Baby" team won three Super Bowls between 1976 and 1983.

# SAN DIEGO CHARGERS

*Los Angeles Chargers (1960)*

*Founded* 1960

*Chargers Hall of Fame*

Frank Buncom, Emil Karas, Bob Laraba, Jacque MacKinnon, Lance
Alworth, Ron Mix, Paul Lowe, Barron Hilton, Keith Lincoln, Ernie
Ladd, Walt Sweeney, John Hadl, Chuck Allen, Gary Garrison, Sid
Gillman, Earl Faison, Dan Fouts, Charlie Joiner, Speedy Duncan,
Russ Washington, Kellen Winslow, George Pernicano, Rolf
Benirschke, Gail Byrd, Gary "Big Hands" Johnson, Doug Wilkerson,
Wes Chandler, Stan Humphries, Bobby Ross, Louie Kelcher, Don
Macek, Ed White, Fred Dean

*Retired Numbers* 14—Dan Fouts; 19—Lance Alworth

*Division/Conference Championships*
6: 1960, 1961, 1963, 1964, 1965, 1994

*AFL Championships* 1: 1963

The Chargers came to the AFL by way of Los Angeles and quickly relocated to their current home, San Diego. Their AFL years saw them as regular contenders, making their way to five of the first six championship games. Unfortunately, their post-merger existence has been less eventful—its highlights limited to an appearance in Super Bowl XXIX, where they lost to the 49ers, and trips to three AFC conference championship games, most recently in 2007, where they fell victim to the Patriots.

## THE RECORDS

LaDainian Tomlinson's 28 rushing touchdowns for the 2006 San Diego Chargers are the most ever by a player in a single season. During the previous two seasons he rushed for a touchdown in 18 consecutive games, also a record.

# TENNESSEE TITANS

*Houston Oilers (1960–1996);*
*Tennessee Oilers (1997–1998)*

*Founded* 1960

## Titans/Oilers Hall of Fame
K. S. "Bud" Adams Jr., Elvin Bethea, George Blanda, Earl Campbell,
Eddie George, Mike Holovak, Ken Houston, Bruce Matthews, Steve
McNair, Warren Moon, Mike Munchak, Jim Norton, Frank Wycheck

## Retired Numbers
1—Warren Moon; 9—Steve McNair; 34—Earl Campbell;
43—Jim Norton; 63—Mike Munchak;
65—Elvin Bethea; 74—Bruce Matthews

## Division/Conference Championships
4: 1960, 1961, 1962, 1999

## AFL Championships 2: 1960, 1961

The Houston Oilers were the AFL's first champions, as the charter team beat the Los Angeles Chargers in 1960 and then beat them again in San Diego for the 1961 title. After losing the all-Texas 1963 AFL Championship to Dallas, the Oilers were a regular presence after the merge—twice coming up against and falling to the Pittsburgh Steelers in the conference championship. After the Oilers relocated to Tennessee in 1997, they were on the winning end of one of the wilder finishes in NFL playoff history. The "Music City Miracle" came against the Buffalo Bills during the Wild Card round of the 1999 playoffs. Down by one point with 16 seconds on the clock, Tennessee's Kevin Dyson took a lateral pass from teammate Frank Wycheck and returned it for a 75-yard touchdown, advancing the Titans deeper into the playoffs, where they eventually lost Super Bowl XXXIV to Kurt Warner and the St. Louis Rams.

# MINNESOTA VIKINGS

## *Founded*
1961

## *Ring of Honor*
Scot Studwell, John Randle, Chuck Foreman, Randall McDaniel,
Jerry Burns, Bill Brown, Cris Carter, Carl Eller, Mick Tingelhoff,
Korey Stringer, Ron Yary, Jim Marshall, Fred Zamberletti, Paul
Krause, Bud Grant, Jim Finks, Alan Page, Fran Tarkenton

## *Retired Numbers*
10—Fran Tarkenton; 53—Mick Tinglehoff; 70—Jim Marshall;
77—Korey Stringer; 80—Chris Carter; 88—Alan Page

## *Conference Championships*
4: 1969, 1973, 1974, 1976

---

### THE RECORDS
Paul Krause (Redskins, Vikings) holds the record for most
career interceptions (81).

---

Minnesota had longed to restore professional football to the area ever since the demise of the Red Jackets. When an ownership group seeking an expansion franchise was denied, an agreement was reached with the AFL to have Minnesota join the new league. Looking to block the upstart league, the NFL quickly reconsidered their rejection and the Vikings were made a part of the NFL. The Vikings played their best football in the 1970s, when Fran Tarkenton led them to three conference championships, ultimately losing out in all three of the Super Bowls they played in—against the Dolphins, Steelers, and Raiders.

# PLAYOFFS: 1933–1965

## 1933

NFL Championship: Chicago Bears 23, New York Giants 21

## 1934

NFL Championship: New York Giants 30, Chicago Bears 13

## 1935

NFL Championship: Detroit Lions 26, New York Giants 7

## 1936

NFL Championship: Green Bay Packers 21, Boston Redskins 6

## 1937

NFL Championship: Washington Redskins 28, Chicago Bears 21

## 1938

NFL Championship: New York Giants 23, Green Bay Packers 17

## 1939

NFL Championship: Green Bay Packers 27, New York Giants 0

## 1940

NFL Championship: Chicago Bears 73, Washington Redskins 0

## 1941

NFL Division Playoff: Chicago Bears 33, Green Bay Packers 14

NFL Championship: Chicago Bears 37, New York Giants 9

## 1942

NFL Championship: Washington Redskins 14, Chicago Bears 6

## 1943

NFL Division Playoff: Washington Redskins 28, New York Giants 0

NFL Championship: Chicago Bears 41, Washington Redskins 21

## 1944

NFL Championship: Green Bay Packers 14, New York Giants 7

## 1945

NFL Championship: Cleveland Rams 15, Washington Redskins 14

## 1946

AAFC Championship: Cleveland Browns 14, New York Yankees 9

NFL Championship: Chicago Bears 24, New York Giants 14

## 1947

NFL Division Playoff: Philadelphia Eagles 21, Pittsburgh Steelers 0

AAFC Championship: Cleveland Browns 14, New York Yankees 3

NFL Championship: Chicago Cardinals 28, Philadelphia Eagles 21

## 1948

AAFC Division Playoff: Buffalo Bills 28, Baltimore Colts 17
AAFC Championship: Cleveland Browns 49, Buffalo Bills 7
NFL Championship: Philadelphia Eagles 7, Chicago Cardinals 0

## 1949

AAFC Semifinal Playoff: Cleveland Browns 31, Buffalo Bills 21
AAFC Semifinal Playoff: San Francisco 49ers 17, Brooklyn/New York
Yankees 7
AAFC Championship: Cleveland Browns 21, San Francisco 49ers 7
NFL Championship: Philadelphia Eagles 14, Los Angeles Rams 0

## 1950

NFL Division Playoff: Cleveland Browns 8, New York Giants 3
NFL Division Playoff: Los Angeles Rams 24, Chicago Bears 14
NFL Championship: Cleveland Browns 30, Los Angeles Rams 28

## 1951

NFL Championship: Los Angeles Rams 24, Cleveland Browns 17

## 1952

NFL Division Playoff: Detroit Lions 31, Los Angeles Rams 21
NFL Championship: Detroit Lions 17, Cleveland Browns 7

## 1953

NFL Championship: Detroit Lions 17, Cleveland Browns 16

## 1954
NFL Championship: Cleveland Browns 56, Detroit Lions 10

## 1955
NFL Championship: Cleveland Browns 38, Los Angeles Rams 14

## 1956
NFL Championship: New York Giants 47, Chicago Bears 7

## 1957
NFL Division Playoff: Detroit Lions 31, San Francisco 49ers 27
NFL Championship: Detroit Lions 59, Cleveland Browns 14

## 1958
NFL Division Playoff: New York Giants 10, Cleveland Browns 0
NFL Championship: Baltimore Colts 23, New York Giants 17 (OT)

## 1959
NFL Championship: Baltimore Colts 31, New York Giants 16

## 1960
AFL Championship: Houston Oilers 24, Los Angeles Chargers 16
NFL Championship: Philadelphia Eagles 17, Green Bay Packers 13

## 1961
AFL Championship: Houston Oilers 10, San Diego Chargers 3
NFL Championship: Green Bay Packers 37, New York Giants 0

## 1962

AFL Championship: Dallas Texans 20, Houston Oilers 17 (OT)
NFL Championship: Green Bay Packers 16, New York Giants 7

## 1963

AFL Divisional Playoff: Boston Patriots 26, Buffalo Bills 8
AFL Championship: San Diego Chargers 51, Boston Patriots 10
NFL Championship: Chicago Bears 14, New York Giants 10

## 1964

AFL Championship: Buffalo Bills 20, San Diego Chargers 7
NFL Championship: Cleveland Browns 27, Baltimore Colts 0

## 1965

NFL Division Playoff: Green Bay Packers 13, Baltimore Colts 10 (OT)
AFL Championship: Buffalo Bills 23, San Diego Chargers 0
NFL Championship: Green Bay Packers 23, Cleveland Browns 12

# ★ 3 ᴿᴰ DOWN ★

# 1966–1989

By 1966, the "war" between the NFL and the AFL had reached a point where together the leagues were spending a combined $7 million to secure their respective draft picks. A merger would prevent the type of bidding wars that had sent salaries out of the owners' control, but when the idea had been floated the previous year, the NFL owners wanted the AFL teams to pay to come aboard, and the AFL balked at the price tag. As players began jumping ship from their respective teams and accepting lucrative offers from outside their league, many of the owners on both sides saw it as an untenable situation. The growing belief was that a merge would strengthen the league as a whole and save those franchises that were struggling financially.

---

### THE RECORDS

On November 27, 1966, the Washington Redskins beat the New York Giants 72-41. The 16 touchdowns scored by both teams and 113 combined points scored still stand today as the most total points and touchdowns recorded in a single game.

---

Cowboys president Tex Schramm arranged for a meeting with AFL founder and Chiefs owner Lamar Hunt. The two laid the groundwork for the merger that would soon follow, and by 1967 there were interleague preseason games, a common draft, and a scheduled AFL–NFL championship game, eventually renamed the Super Bowl after an off-hand comment by Hunt stuck. The name wasn't to the liking of everyone; Pete Rozelle, who had been selected to stay on as commissioner of the merged league, hated the term "Super" and tried to find an alternative before accepting that the name had caught on and he was stuck with it.

The merger would still require maneuvers both in and outside the league. Outside the league, the merger needed to clear Congress, which it did after Rozelle promised Senator Russell Long of Louisiana that New Orleans would be granted the newly merged league's first expansion franchise. Within the league, things would proceed as they had for the next three seasons, with pre- and post-season meetings between the two leagues. Two conferences would be created and installed for the 1970 season, when the merger would be completed—the National Football Conference (NFC) and the American Football Conference (AFC). Realignment would follow, and with it the moving of the Steelers, Colts, and Browns into the AFC to create two equal groupings. On the NFC side, divisional realignment was contentious and was not completed until Rozelle dropped five pieces of paper into a bowl, each with a different plan on it, and had his secretary pick the winner.

The Super Bowl era began with a continuation of Green Bay's dominant run as the class of the NFL, taking the first two championships, with the title trophy eventually being named after their legendary coach—Vince Lombardi. The road to the second Green Bay Super Bowl was paved in ice, as temperatures at kickoff were 13 degrees below zero and falling. Lambeau Field's heating grid had not been designed for temperatures that low, and anything it managed to melt only froze over, creating a hazard that required the entire system to be shut down. Stories from the frozen tundra include NFL Films soundmen taken to the hospital, frozen whistles, and frozen coffee cups. Camera wheels froze, preventing their operators from focusing, but enough of them remained operational to catch the Packers' 21-17 victory in what would later be called "The Ice Bowl."

The following season saw more hijinks on the road to the Super Bowl. In a key AFL matchup between the Jets and the Oakland Raiders, both of whom would go on to meet again in the conference championship game, a network miscue caused the game's broadcast to be dumped in favor of the scheduled airing of *Heidi*. The deluge of phone calls from angry fans to the station made it impossible for management to get through on the switchboard and straighten everything out. What most of the viewing public missed was a furious Oakland comeback, during which the game swung from a 32-29 Jet lead to a 43-32 Oakland victory. But the Jets would get the better of Oakland when it counted, beating them in the championship and advancing to Super Bowl III, where their improbable win gave the AFL portion of the merged league some much-needed credibility.

## THE RECORDS

Tom Dempsey set the mark for the longest field goal ever kicked when he converted a 63-yarder for New Orleans on November 8, 1970, in a game against the Lions. The feat has since been matched by Denver's Jason Elam and Oakland's Sebastian Janikowski.

After the merger was announced, New Orleans, Atlanta, Cincinnati, and Miami joined the league. As the end of the 1960s and early 1970s saw success in Baltimore, Dallas, Minnesota, and Kansas City, it was the Dolphins who were poised to become the next great NFL team. Coached by Don Shula, the Dolphins would follow a loss in the 1971 Super Bowl to the Cowboys with arguably the greatest season in NFL history: fourteen regular season victories, zero losses, and a clean run through the playoffs to give the 'Fins their first championship and the only perfect season in the history of the game. They followed it up with another Super Bowl in 1973 before falling to the Raiders in the 1974 playoffs.

## THE RECORDS
The 1978 Patriots rushed for 3,165 yards—the most ever in a single season.

At the midpoint of the decade, the league was ready to expand again, with new franchises in Seattle and Tampa Bay, and a new powerhouse emerged as a steel curtain came crashing down on the NFL. For the next six seasons Chuck Noll navigated a group that featured the likes of Terry Bradshaw, Franco Harris, and Lynn Swann to dynasty status, taking four Super Bowls in four attempts. The end of the decade ushered in the Wild Card era, Al Davis's innovation from the AFL in which the best second-place teams were admitted into an expanded playoff format.

## THE RECORDS

On December 7, 1980, the San Francisco 49ers trailed
the New Orleans Saints 35-7 at the half. San Fran would go on
a 28-point second-half run to tie the score and complete
the comeback with an overtime field goal—the largest deficit
ever overcome to win a game.

After a work stoppage shortened the 1982 season (and a lockout resulted in the brief adaption of replacement players in 1987), the remainder of the eighties featured several teams jockeying for supremacy, with the Broncos repeatedly failing to clear their Super Bowl hurdle as they were thwarted by the Redskins, Giants, and 49ers— arguably the most dominant franchise of the era. The most dominant *team*, however, was Mike Ditka's 1985 Bears. Aggressive and brash, they excelled on both sides of the ball, leading the league in interceptions; points, yards, and number of first downs allowed; rushing yards and touchdowns gained on offense and denied on defense; and turnovers caused. William "Refrigerator" Perry, Mike Singletary, and Jim McMahon became household names, and Walter Payton put the cherry on top of his Hall of Fame career as the Bears marched across the NFL to the tune of a 15-1 record and a win in Super Bowl XX.

# WALTER PAYTON:
## Sweetness

Walter Payton rushed for more than 3,500 yards in college, his 65 touchdowns an NCAA record. His entire NFL career was played in Chicago with the Bears, for whom he scored 125 touchdowns and gained a combined 21,803 net yards. In 1977 he led the league in all-purpose yards, touchdowns, rushing yards, and yards from scrimmage, among other categories.

The nine-time Pro Bowl player once held the single-game record for on-the-ground performance, having rushed for 275 yards. When Payton retired, he did so with a back pocket full of additional league records, including career rushing yards, touchdowns, carries, yards from scrimmage, and all-purpose yards. His coach, Mike Ditka, referred to him as the greatest football player he had ever seen.

## THE RECORDS
From 1982 to 1983 the San Diego Chargers played eleven consecutive games in which they gained 400 or more yards—the longest streak of its kind.

# ATLANTA FALCONS

*Founded* 1966

*Ring of Honor*

Tommy Nobis, Jeff Van Note, Steve Bartowski, William Andrews,
Jessie Tuggle, Claude Humphrey, Mike Kenn, Deion Sanders

*Conference Championships* 1: 1998

The Atlanta Falcons were on their way to becoming the first AFL expansion franchise since the charter class of 1960; all that was required of them was to secure the rights to play in Atlanta–Fulton County Stadium. Instead, NFL Commissioner Pete Rozelle swooped in and made a deal for the stadium on behalf of the league and found an investment group to back it. It would take the team a little over a decade to make the playoffs, but it would be another twenty years on top of that before the Falcons had any real impact on the league, when the "Dirty Birds" danced their way to the Super Bowl. The twenty-first century Falcons had some additional success with quarterback Mike Vick, including two trips to the playoffs, each with a win—the 2004 team advancing to the NFC conference championship. Vick was let go after he pled guilty to dog fighting, but the team pushed forward, returning to the playoffs in 2008 and securing a first-round playoff bye in 2010 before losing to the eventual Super Bowl Champion Green Bay Packers.

# MIAMI DOLPHINS

*Founded* 1966

## *Honor Roll*

Joe Robbie, Larry Csonka, Bob Griese, Jim Langer, Paul Warfield, Nick Buoniconti, 1972 Undefeated Team, Larry Little, Dwight Stephenson, Bob Kuechenberg, Dwight Stephenson, Don Shula, Nat Moore, Dan Marino, Mark Clayton, Mark Duper, Dick Anderson, Richmond Webb, Bob Baumhower, Doug Beters, Jake Scott, Bill Stanfill, Jim Mandich

## *Retired Numbers*

12—Bob Griese; 13—Dan Marino; 39—Larry Csonka

## *Conference Championships*

5: 1971, 1972, 1973, 1982, 1984

## *Super Bowl Victories*

2: Super Bowl VII (1972), Super Bowl VIII (1973)

## THE RECORDS

Dan Marino led the league in passing six times, from 1984 to 1986, and again in 1988, 1992, and 1997. Marino also led the league in passing yards gained five times (a record he shares with Sonny Jurgensen), passed for 5,084 yards in 1984, and had thirteen games in which he passed for more than 400 yards (four times in the 1984 season, three times in 1986)—both records. Along with Peyton Manning, his six four-touchdown games in a single season are the most ever recorded by a quarterback.

The Dolphins' creation was the final salvo in the AFL/NFL franchise wars. After the AFL was rebuffed by an Atlanta group for the franchise that would eventually become the Falcons, they awarded a team to Miami, returning professional sports to the Sunshine State for the first time since the AAFC. Head coach Don Shula would depart Baltimore after losing Super Bowl III and have an immediate effect on the team, seeing them through their historic run that included two Super Bowl victories and a perfect season. In the 1980s, Shula paired with quarterback Dan Marino, and while the two could not bring another title to Miami, they were twice AFC champions and perennial contenders.

# NEW ORLEANS SAINTS

*Founded* 1967

## Saints Hall of Fame

Archie Manning, Danny Abramowicz, Tommy Myers, Tom Dempsey,
Billy Kilmer, Derland Moore, Tony Galbreath, George Rogers,
Jake Kupp, John Hill, Joe Federspiel, Jim Finks, Henry Childs, Bob
Pollard, Doug Atkins, Dave Whitsell, Dave Waymer, Rickey Jackson,
Stan Brock, Dalton Hilliard, Sam Mills, Bobby Hebert, Eric Martin,
Vaughan Johnson, Pat Swilling, Hoby Brenner, Jim Wilks, Jim Mora,
Frank Warren, Wayne Martin, Jim Dombrowski, Rueben Mayes,
Steve Sidwell, Joel Hilgenberg, Joe Johnson, Willie Roaf, Morten
Andersen, Joe Horn

## Retired Numbers 31—Jim Taylor; 51—Sam Mills;
57—Rickey Jackson; 81—Doug Atkins

## Conference Championships
1: 2009

## Super Bowl Victories
1: Super Bowl XLIV (2009)

## THE RECORDS

Morten Andersen, kicker for the Saints, Falcons, Giants, Chiefs, and Vikings, has scored 2,544 total points in his career, the most ever by a player. Andersen played from 1982 to 2007 and made 565 field goals along with 849 points after touchdowns (PATs) to reach his mark.

The Saints were promised into the league as part of the political maneuvering that allowed the AFL/NFL merger to clear the U.S. Congress. The only real bright spot in their first twenty years of play was quarterback Archie Manning, who held a franchise record for passing yards until it was broken by Drew Brees in 2011. Following the devastation of Hurricane Katrina, during which the Saints' home stadium was used as a shelter, the 2009 Saints helped recharge their hometown fans with a playoff run that was capped off with a Super Bowl win.

# CINCINNATI BENGALS

*Founded* 1968

*Retired Numbers* 54—Bob Johnson

*Conference Championships* 2: 1982, 1988

Cincinnati's greatest contribution to the NFL's legacy is not its two conference championships, each resulting in a Super Bowl loss to the 49ers. Under owner/head coach Paul Brown and his assistant Bill Walsh, the Bengals implemented what would later be regarded as the first use of the West Coast offense—a system that hinged on a mobile and accurate quarterback who could make short, quick passes. Walsh would adapt it to his 49er teams in the eighties.

# SEATTLE SEAHAWKS

*Founded* 1976

*Ring of Honor*

Dave Brown, Kenny Easley, Jacob Green, Pete Gross, Cortez Kennedy,
Chuck Knox, Dave Krieg, Steve Largent, Curt Warner, Jim Zorn

*Retired Numbers*

12—"Fans/The Twelfth Man"; 71—Walter Jones; 80—Steve Largent

*Conference Championships*

1: 2005

The Seahawks entered the NFL as an NFC team and switched conferences with the Bucs in their second season. The team's history was uneventful until they moved from the Kingdome to their current home. While many teams have taken to honoring their fans as the "twelfth man," the Seahawks have true reason to do so, as their home field has been measured as one of the loudest in professional sports. The advantage it provides was most clearly displayed in 2005, when the Seahawks won their first home playoff game in more than twenty years and followed it up with a second win in the conference championship against Carolina to advance to the Super Bowl. The Seahawks could not get past Pittsburgh but returned to the playoffs three more times to close out the decade, each time making it past the first round.

# TAMPA BAY BUCCANEERS

*Founded* 1976

*Ring of Honor*
Lee Roy Selmon, John McKay, Jimmie Giles

*Retired Numbers*
63—Lee Roy Selmon

*Conference Championships* 1: 2002

*Super Bowl Victories* 1: Super Bowl XXXVII (2002)

---

### THE RECORDS

From 1976 to 1977 the Tampa Bay Buccaneers lost 26 consecutive games (including the entire 1976 season)—the longest consecutive losing streak to date.

---

The Bucs lost their first twenty-six games after being expanded into the league in 1976, going perfectly winless in their inaugural season (playing in the AFC) and losing all but the final two games of the 1977 season after moving over to the NFC. Although the franchise was able to put together a few positive years at the turn of the decade, including a trip to the 1979 conference championship game, most of Tampa Bay's first two decades of professional play were marred with losing efforts, including fourteen consecutive seasons under .500. In an effort to at least share the misery, the Bucs chose to wear white uniforms at home, forcing visiting teams to wear darker colors that would potentially absorb more Florida sun.

The sun finally began to shine on the Bucs during the late 1990s, when the team once again started making it to the playoffs, advancing to the divisional round in 1997 and the conference championship in 1999. In 2002, under head coach Jon Gruden, Tampa Bay bested Gruden's former team, the Raiders, in Super Bowl XXXVII—dubbed the "Pirate Bowl."

# POSTSEASON: 1966–1989

## *1966*

AFL Conference Championship: Kansas City Chiefs 31, Buffalo Bills 7

NFL Conference Championship: Green Bay Packers 34, Dallas Cowboys 27

Super Bowl I: Green Bay Packers 35, Kansas City Chiefs 10

## *1967*

NFL Division: Green Bay Packers 28, Los Angeles Rams 7

NFL Division: Dallas Cowboys 52, Cleveland Browns 14

AFL Conference Championship: Oakland Raiders 40, Houston Oilers 7

NFL Conference Championship: Green Bay Packers 21, Dallas Cowboys 17

Super Bowl II: Green Bay Packers 33, Oakland Raiders 14

---

**THE RECORDS**

Two players hold the record for most field goals kicked in a Super
Bowl (4): Don Chandler with Green Bay in Super Bowl II and
Ray Wersching with San Francisco in Super Bowl XVI.

---

## *1968*

AFL Division: Oakland Raiders 41, Kansas City Chiefs 6

NFL Division: Cleveland Browns 31, Dallas Cowboys 20

NFL Division: Baltimore Colts 24, Minnesota Vikings 14

AFL Conference Championship: New York Jets 27, Oakland Raiders 23

NFL Conference Championship: Baltimore Colts 34, Cleveland Browns 0

Super Bowl III: New York Jets 16, Baltimore Colts 7

## 1969

AFL Division: Oakland Raiders 56, Houston Oilers 7

AFL Division: Kansas City Chiefs 13, New York Jets 6

NFL Division: Cleveland Browns 38, Dallas Cowboys 14

NFL Division: Minnesota Vikings 23, Los Angeles Rams 20

AFL Conference Championship: Kansas City Chiefs 17, Oakland Raiders 7

NFL Conference Championship: Minnesota Vikings 27, Cleveland Browns 7

Super Bowl IV: Kansas City Chiefs 23, Minnesota Vikings 7

## 1970

AFC Division: Baltimore Colts 17, Cincinnati Bengals 0

AFC Division: Oakland Raiders 21, Miami Dolphins 14

NFC Division: Dallas Cowboys 5, Detroit Lions 0

NFC Division: San Francisco 49ers 17, Minnesota Vikings 14

AFC Conference Championship: Baltimore Colts 27, Oakland Raiders 17

NFC Conference Championship: Dallas Cowboys 17, San Francisco 49ers 10

Super Bowl V: Baltimore Colts 16, Dallas Cowboys 13

## 1971

AFC Division: Baltimore Colts 20, Cleveland Browns 3

AFC Division: Miami Dolphins 27, Kansas City Chiefs 24 (OT)

NFC Division: San Francisco 49ers 24, Washington Redskins 20

NFC Division: Dallas Cowboys 20, Minnesota Vikings 12

AFC Conference Championship: Miami Dolphins 21, Baltimore Colts 0

NFC Conference Championship: Dallas Cowboys 14, San Francisco 49ers 3

Super Bowl VI: Dallas Cowboys 24, Miami Dolphins 3

# *1972*

AFC Division: Miami Dolphins 20, Cleveland Browns 14

AFC Division: Pittsburgh Steelers 13, Oakland Raiders 7

NFC Division: Washington Redskins 16, Green Bay Packers 3

NFC Division: Dallas Cowboys 30, San Francisco 49ers 28

AFC Conference Championship: Miami Dolphins 21, Pittsburgh Steelers 17

NFC Conference Championship:

Washington Redskins 26, Dallas Cowboys 3

Super Bowl VII: Miami Dolphins 14, Washington Redskins 7

---

## THE RECORDS

While former head coach Don Shula insists that his 1972 Miami Dolphins don't have annual champagne parties to mark the falling of each new season's last undefeated team, the Dolphins 14-0 regular-season record and 3-0 run through the postseason, capped with a victory in Super Bowl VII, stands as the only perfect season in NFL history. To borrow from Miami running back Mercury Morris, two other teams have made appearances on the Dolphins' "block" without ever getting the furniture off the truck: the 1942 Bears (11-0) and 2007 Patriots (16-0) both went undefeated in the regular season, only to fall short in their respective championship games.

---

# *1973*

AFC Division: Miami Dolphins 34, Cincinnati Bengals 16

AFC Division: Oakland Raiders 33, Pittsburgh Steelers 14

NFC Division: Minnesota Viking 27, Washington Redskins 20

NFC Division: Dallas Cowboys 27, Los Angeles Rams 16

AFC Conference Championship: Miami Dolphins 27, Oakland Raiders 10

NFC Conference Championship: Minnesota Vikings 27, Dallas Cowboys 10
Super Bowl VIII: Miami Dolphins 24, Minnesota Vikings 7

## *1974*

AFC Division: Pittsburgh Steelers 32, Buffalo Bulls 14
AFC Division: Oakland Raiders 28, Miami Dolphins 26
NFC Division: Los Angeles Rams 19, Washington Redskins 10
NFC Division: Minnesota Vikings 30, St. Louis Cardinals 14
AFC Conference Championship: Pittsburgh Steelers 24, Oakland Raiders 13
NFC Conference Championship: Minnesota Vikings 14, Los Angeles Rams 10
Super Bowl IX: Pittsburgh Steelers 16, Minnesota Vikings 6

## *1975*

AFC Division: Oakland Raiders 31, Cincinnati Bengals 28
AFC Division: Pittsburgh Steelers 28, Baltimore Colts 10
NFC Division: Los Angeles Rams 35, St. Louis Cardinals 23
NFC Division: Dallas Cowboys 17, Minnesota Vikings 14
AFC Conference Championship: Pittsburgh Steelers 24, Oakland Raiders 10
NFC Conference Championship: Dallas Cowboys 37, Los Angeles Rams 7
Super Bowl X: Pittsburgh Steelers 21, Dallas Cowboys 17

## *1976*

AFC Division: Pittsburgh Steelers 40, Baltimore Colts 14
AFC Division: Oakland Raiders 24, New England Patriots 21
NFC Division: Minnesota Vikings 35, Washington Redskins 20
NFC Division: Los Angeles Rams 14, Dallas Cowboys 12
AFC Conference Championship: Oakland Raiders 24, Pittsburgh Steelers 7

NFC Conference Championship: Minnesota Vikings 24, Los Angeles Rams 13

Super Bowl XI: Oakland Raiders 32, Minnesota Vikings 14

## *1977*

AFC Division: Denver Broncos 34, Pittsburgh Steelers 21

AFC Division: Oakland Raiders 37, Baltimore Colts 31 (OT)

NFC Division: Dallas Cowboys 37, Chicago Bears 7

NFC Division: Minnesota Vikings 14, Los Angeles Rams 7

AFC Conference Championship: Denver Broncos 20, Oakland Raiders 17

NFC Conference Championship: Dallas Cowboys 23, Minnesota Vikings 6

Super Bowl XII: Dallas Cowboys 27, Denver Broncos 10

## *1978*

AFC Wild Card: Houston Oilers 17, Miami Dolphins 9

NFC Wild Card: Atlanta Falcons 14, Philadelphia Eagles 13

AFC Division: Pittsburgh Steelers 33, Denver Broncos 10

AFC Division: Houston Oilers 31, New England Patriots 14

NFC Division: Dallas Cowboys 27, Atlanta Falcons 20

NFC Division: Los Angeles Rams 34, Minnesota Vikings 10

AFC Conference Championship: Pittsburgh Steelers 34, Houston Oilers 5

NFC Conference Championship: Dallas Cowboys 28, Los Angeles Rams 0

Super Bowl XIII: Pittsburgh Steelers 35, Dallas Cowboys 31

---

### THE RECORDS

Franco Harris rushed for 354 yards in four Super Bowls for
the Pittsburgh Steelers, the most career yards gained on the ground
in the big game.

---

# *1979*

AFC Wild Card: Houston Oilers 13, Denver Broncos 7

NFC Wild Card: Philadelphia Eagles 27, Chicago Bears 17

AFC Division: Pittsburgh Steelers 34, Miami Dolphins 14

AFC Division: Houston Oilers 17, San Diego Chargers 14

NFC Division: Los Angeles Rams 21, Dallas Cowboys 19

NFC Division: Tampa Bay Buccaneers 24, Philadelphia Eagles 17

AFC Conference Championship: Pittsburgh Steelers 27, Houston Oilers 13

NFC Conference Championship:

Los Angeles Rams 9, Tampa Bay Buccaneers 0

Super Bowl XIV: Pittsburgh Steelers 31, Los Angeles Rams 19

---

### THE RECORDS

Chuck Noll has more Super Bowl wins than any other coach, having led the Pittsburgh Steelers to the promised land four times (1974, 1975, 1978, and 1979). Including pre-merger championships, Noll is tied for third all-time with Guy Chamberlain; he trails Vince Lombardi, Curly Lambeau, and George Halas (6).

---

# *1980*

AFC Wild Card: Oakland Raiders 27, Houston Oilers 7

NFC Wild Card: Dallas Cowboys 34, Los Angeles Rams 13

AFC Division: San Diego Chargers 20, Buffalo Bills 14

AFC Division: Oakland Raiders 14, Cleveland Browns 12

NFC Division: Dallas Cowboys 30, Atlanta Falcons 27

NFC Division: Philadelphia Eagles 31, Minnesota Vikings 16

AFC Conference Championship: Oakland Raiders 34, San Diego Chargers 27

NFC Conference Championship: Philadelphia Eagles 20, Dallas Cowboys 7
Super Bowl XV: Oakland Raiders 27, Philadelphia Eagles 10

## *1981*

AFC Wild Card: Buffalo Bills 31, New York Jets 27
NFC Wild Card: New York Giants 27, Philadelphia Eagles 21
AFC Division: Cincinnati Bengals 28, Buffalo Bills 21
AFC Division: San Diego Chargers 41, Miami Dolphins 38 (OT)
NFC Division: San Francisco 49ers 38, New York Giants 24
NFC Division: Dallas Cowboys 38, Tampa Bay Buccaneers 0
AFC Conference Championship:
Cincinnati Bengals 27, San Diego Chargers 7
NFC Conference Championship: San Francisco 49ers 28, Dallas Cowboys 27
Super Bowl XVI: San Francisco 49ers 26, Cincinnati Bengals 21

## *1982*

AFC Wild Card: New York Jets 44, Cincinnati Bengals 17
AFC Wild Card: Los Angeles Raiders 27, Cleveland Browns 10
AFC Wild Card: Miami Dolphins 28, New England Patriots 13
AFC Wild Card: San Diego Chargers 31, Pittsburgh Steelers 28
NFC Wild Card: Washington Redskins 31, Detroit Lions 7
NFC Wild Card: Green Bay Packers 41, St. Louis Cardinals 16
NFC Wild Card: Minnesota Vikings 30, Atlanta Falcons 24
NFC Wild Card: Dallas Cowboys 30, Tampa Bay Buccaneers 17
AFC Division: Miami Dolphins 34, San Diego Chargers 13
AFC Division: New York Jets 17, Los Angeles Raiders 14
NFC Division: Washington Redskins 21, Minnesota Vikings 7

NFC Division: Dallas Cowboys 37, Green Bay Packers 26
AFC Conference Championship: Miami Dolphins 14, New York Jets 0
NFC Conference Championship:
Washington Redskins 31, Dallas Cowboys 17
Super Bowl XVII: Washington Redskins 27, Miami Dolphins 17

## *1983*

AFC Wild Card: Seattle Seahawks 31, Denver Broncos 7
NFC Wild Card: Los Angeles Rams 24, Dallas Cowboys 17
AFC Division: Seattle Seahawks 27, Miami Dolphins 20
AFC Division: Los Angeles Raiders 38, Pittsburgh Steelers10
NFC Division: Washington Redskin 51, Los Angeles Rams 7
NFC Division: San Francisco 49ers 24, Detroit Lions 23
AFC Conference Championship: Los Angeles Raiders 30, Seattle Seahawks 14
NFC Conference Championship:
Washington Redskins 24, San Francisco 49ers 21
Super Bowl XVIII: Los Angeles Raiders 38, Washington Redskins 9

## *1984*

AFC Wild Card: Seattle Seahawks 13, Los Angeles Raiders 7
NFC Wild Card: New York Giants 16, Los Angeles Rams 13
AFC Division: Pittsburgh Steelers 24, Denver Broncos 17
AFC Division: Miami Dolphins 31, Seattle Seahawks 10
NFC Division: Chicago Bears 23, Washington Redskins 19
NFC Division: San Francisco 49ers 21, New York Giants 10
AFC Conference Championship: Miami Dolphins 45, Pittsburgh Steelers 28
NFC Conference Championship: San Francisco 49ers 23, Chicago Bears 0
Super Bowl XIX: San Francisco 49ers 38, Miami Dolphins 16

# MARCUS ALLEN

University of Southern California's Marcus Allen was the first college player to rush for more than 2,000 yards in a single season. The Heisman Trophy winner led the country in scoring and was drafted by the Raiders in 1982. Allen's impact was immediately felt, as his Offensive Rookie of the Year season would include 697 yards on the ground and see the Raiders to the playoffs. Allen topped 1,000 yards the next three seasons, rushing for 1,759 and earning MVP honors in 1985. His 74-yard touchdown run in Super Bowl XVIII stood as the longest in Super Bowl history for more than twenty-five years and helped earn him Super Bowl MVP honors.

A contentious relationship with owner Al Davis eventually prompted Allen to leave the Raiders, and in 1993 he went to the Chiefs. The Comeback Player of the Year, Allen led the AFC in touchdowns and continued to lead the team in rushing yardage every year thereafter, until his final season in 1997. He retired as the first player in NFL history to rush for more than 10,000 yards while also receiving for more than 5,000. He finished his career with eleven playoff touchdowns, averaging five yards per playoff carry.

# 1985

AFC Wild Card: New England Patriots 26, New York Jets 14

NFC Wild Card: New York Giants 17, San Francisco 49ers 3

AFC Division: Miami Dolphins 24, Cleveland Browns 21

AFC Division: New England Patriots 27, Los Angeles Raiders 20

NFC Division: Chicago Bears 21, New York Giants 0

NFC Division: Los Angeles Rams 20, Dallas Cowboys 0

AFC Conference Championship:
New England Patriots 31, Miami Dolphins 14

NFC Conference Championship: Chicago Bears 24, Los Angeles Rams 0

Super Bowl XX: Chicago Bears 46, New England Patriots 10

# 1986

AFC Wild Card: New York Jets 35, Kansas City Chiefs 15

NFC Wild Card: Washington Redskins 19, Los Angeles Rams 7

AFC Division: Cleveland Browns 23, New York Jets 20 (OT)

AFC Division: Denver Broncos 22, New England Patriots 17

NFC Division: Washington Redskins 27, Chicago Bears 13

NFC Division: New York Giants 49, San Francisco 49ers 3

AFC Conference Championship:
Denver Broncos 23, Cleveland Browns 20 (OT)

NFC Conference Championship:
New York Giants 17, Washington Redskins 0

Super Bowl XXI: New York Giants 39, Denver Broncos 20

# LAWRENCE TAYLOR

Lawrence Taylor is credited with redefining the defensive game from the outside linebacker position. Selected first in the 1981 draft by the New York Giants (second overall), LT was a force to be reckoned with. His leg-breaking hit against Redskins quarterback Joe Theismann on Monday Night Football was the sort of career highlight that kept opposing teams up at night during the week leading up to a game against the Giants—they had no choice but to address the runaway train that was repeatedly set to destroy their offensive line.

The NFL Defensive Player of the Year in 1981, 1982, and 1986, Taylor was selected to 10 Pro Bowls and in 1986 became the first defensive player in 15 years to be named league MVP after recording 20.5 sacks, 105 tackles, and 2 forced fumbles. His career saw two Super Bowl Championships for the Giants, and added up to 33 forced fumbles, 10 fumble recoveries, 1,088 tackles, and 132.5 sacks—second all-time at retirement (not including the 9.5 he would have had in 1981 had the stat been recognized).

## THE RECORDS

Phil Simms made 22 of 25 passes (88 percent) for the New York Giants (including 10 consecutive completions) in Super Bowl XXI, the highest completion percentage by a Super Bowl quarterback.

# *1987*

AFC Wild Card: Houston Oilers 23, Seattle Seahawks 20 (OT)

NFC Wild Card: Minnesota Vikings 44, New Orleans Saints 10

AFC Division: Cleveland Browns 38, Indianapolis Colts 21

AFC Division: Denver Broncos 34, Houston Oilers 10

NFC Division: Washington Redskins 21, Chicago Bears 17

NFC Division: Minnesota Vikings 36, San Francisco 49ers 24

AFC Conference Championship: Denver Broncos 38, Cleveland Browns 33

NFC Conference Championship:
Washington Redskins 17, Minnesota Vikings 10

Super Bowl XXII: Washington Redskins 42, Denver Broncos 10

---

## THE RECORDS

Timmy Smith rushed for 204 yards for the Washington Redskins against the Denver Broncos in Super Bowl XXII—the most by any player in a Super Bowl.

---

# *1988*

AFC Wild Card: Houston Oilers 24, Cleveland Browns 23

NFC Wild Card: Minnesota Vikings 28, Los Angeles Rams 17

AFC Division: Buffalo Bills 17, Houston Oilers 10

AFC Division: Cincinnati Bengals 21, Seattle Seahawks 13

NFC Division: Chicago Bears 20, Philadelphia Eagles 12

NFC Division: San Francisco 49ers 34, Minnesota Vikings 9

AFC Conference Championship: Cincinnati Bengals 21, Buffalo Bills 10

NFC Conference Championship: San Francisco 49ers 28, Chicago Bears 3

Super Bowl XXIII: San Francisco 49ers 20, Cincinnati Bengals 16

## *1989*

AFC Wild Card: Pittsburgh Steelers 26, Houston Oilers 23 (OT)

NFC Wild Card: Los Angeles Rams 21, Philadelphia Eagles 7

AFC Division: Cleveland Browns 34, Buffalo Bills 30

AFC Division: Denver Broncos 24, Pittsburgh Steelers 23

NFC Division: Los Angeles Rams 19, New York Giants 13 (OT)

NFC Division: San Francisco 49ers 41, Minnesota Vikings 13

AFC Conference Championship: Denver Broncos 37, Cleveland Browns 21

NFC Conference Championship:
San Francisco 49ers 30, Los Angeles Rams 3

Super Bowl XXIV: San Francisco 49ers 55, Denver Broncos 10

# ★ 4$^{TH}$ DOWN ★

----------------

# 1990–2010

The 1990s saw the league expand and modify its playoff format to accommodate the admittance of the Carolina Panthers and Jacksonville Jaguars into the league. By the middle of the decade each conference would have four divisions from which six teams would advance to the playoffs. Additional franchise shuffling saw the Raiders move back to Oakland, the Oilers to Tennessee, the Rams to St. Louis, and the Cleveland Browns moved to Baltimore where they were reborn as the Ravens, with a new Browns team admitted to the league as an expansion franchise a few years later.

The last decade of the twentieth century was one in which the Bills became a dominant force in the AFC, the Cowboys reemerged as world champions, and the torch was passed in San Francisco from Joe Montana

---

### THE RECORDS

On November 13, 1994, Drew Bledsoe of the New England Patriots completed 45 passes against the Minnesota Vikings in an overtime game. Not only was this the most completions by a team, but combined with Warren Moon's 26 passes for the Vikings, it was the most ever in a game. Bledsoe's 70 pass attempts without an interception is also a record.

to Steve Young—who continued to pass the ball to Jerry Rice all the way to the Super Bowl. At the end of the decade, as a new guard of elite quarterbacks was ready to emerge, a former supermarket shelf stocker who had washed out of Packers' training camp and was languishing in the Arena Football League would set the league on fire.

Making his way back to the pros by way of the NFL's European league, Kurt Warner became the second-string quarterback in St. Louis and was thrust into the spotlight when starter Trent Green tore his ACL during the preseason. What followed was the stuff of legend, as Warner, along with Marshall Faulk and a receiving corps that included Isaac Bruce, Torry Holt, and Az-Zahir Hakim, put on a clinic for the rest of the league. Throwing for more than 4,000 yards and 41 touchdowns, Warner completed over 65 percent of his passes in a magical season that reached its apex at Super Bowl XXXIV. There, Warner threw two touchdown passes, including a 75-yard bomb to Isaac Bruce that gave the Rams the lead with less than two minutes to play. It was a season for the ages, and Warner followed it up over the next two, returning the Rams to the Super Bowl in 2001. Unfortunately for the Rams, at that point the new elite in the NFL had arrived.

---

### THE RECORDS

The 2000 Rams were the "Greatest Show on Turf," gaining 7,075 yards—the most ever in a single season.

---

The first decade of the twenty-first century saw another classic quarterback rivalry emerge, as the Patriots' Tom Brady and the Colts' Peyton Manning took their place among the most celebrated within the game. Brady's Patriots took on dynasty status, and in the process twice moved on in the playoffs at the expense of Manning's Colts. The Colts finally got the upper hand in 2006, besting New England in the playoffs en route to a victory in Super Bowl XLI.

The last half of the decade was one in which the quarterback crop of 2004 bore significant fruit, as Ben Roethlisberger led the Steelers to two more titles, Eli Manning led the Giants to their third, and Phillip Rivers made strides in turning the corner for San Diego. Rivers' emergence with the Chargers displaced San Diego quarterback Drew Brees, who took the New Orleans Saints to their first title in 2009. The decade closed with the 45th Super Bowl, featuring two classic teams in Pittsburgh and Green Bay, and the promise of a new era of greatness. Packers quarterback Aaron Rodgers, the forever understudy of Brett Favre, finally got the chance to step into his own, and did so with an MVP performance that brought one more title to Titletown and planted the seeds for the next generation of NFL legends.

---

### THE RECORDS

Adrian Peterson's 296 yards gained on the ground for Minnesota in a 2007 game against San Diego is the most rushing yards gained by a player in a single game.

---

### THE RECORDS

The 2008 Indianapolis Colts beat the New England Patriots 18-15 on November 2, beginning a 23-game winning streak that stands as the longest in NFL history. They would not lose again until December 27 of the following year, when the New York Jets beat them 29-15.

# CAROLINA PANTHERS

*Founded* 1995

*Hall of Honor*
Mike McCormack, Sam Mills, PSL Owners

*Retired Number* 51—Sam Mills

*Conference Championships* 1: 2003

In 1995, after a lengthy selection process, the Carolina Panthers took the field as one of two new expansion franchises—the first additions to the NFL in almost twenty years. The team hit the ground running, making it to the conference championship in its second year with coach Dom Capers and quarterback Kerry Collins. The immediate success was short lived but in 2002 the team picked former Giants defensive coordinator John Fox to take over as head coach. Within a year they advanced to their first Super Bowl, where they ran into the New England Patriots and battled them to the end, losing on a 41-yard field goal with only four seconds left on the clock. Halftime wardrobe malfunction aside, it has been recognized by some sportswriters as one of the greatest Super Bowls ever played.

# JACKSONVILLE JAGUARS

*Founded* 1995

*Pride of the Jaguars* Tony Boselli

*Best Season*
1999 (14-2), lost AFC conference championship

The second of two expansion teams to enter the league in 1995, the Jaguars' brief existence has been less eventful than their expansion-mates, the Panthers. Like Carolina, Jacksonville did advance to the conference championship in their second year, but the team has yet to secure the AFC crown, and its chief accomplishment on the field was its 1999 campaign where the Jags again advanced to the conference championship before losing to the Titans.

# BALTIMORE RAVENS

*Founded* 1996

*Ring of Honor*

Earnest Byner, Peter Boulware, Jonathan Ogden, Michael McCrary,
Matt Stover, Art Modell, Johnny Unitas, the Baltimore Colts

*Conference Championships* 1: 2000

*Super Bowl Victories*

1: Super Bowl XXXV (2000)

The Baltimore Ravens (named for Baltimore's Edgar Allen Poe and his famous work) are really the Cleveland Browns in disguise, but tradition won out when the city of Cleveland was granted the right to preserve its history and tack it on to a new team once it arrived—which it did in 1999. In fifteen years of play the Ravens have established a genuine history of their own, built on defensive excellence. They capitalized on their strength in their one and only Super Bowl appearance, beating the New York Giants 34-7 in 2000. Since then the Ravens have made several trips back to the playoffs, getting as deep as the conference championship in 2008.

# HOUSTON TEXANS

*Founded* 2002

*Best Season*
2009, second place AFC South (9-7)

The last NFL expansion team to date, the Texans' short history has yet to include a playoff appearance. Through 2010 they had three non-losing seasons, one of them with a winning record.

# POSTSEASON: 1990–2010

## *1990*

AFC Wild Card: Cincinnati Bengals 41, Houston Oilers 14

AFC Wild Card: Miami Dolphins 17, Kansas City Chiefs 16

NFC Wild Card: Washington Redskins 20, Philadelphia Eagles 6

NFC Wild Card: Chicago Bears 16, New Orleans Saints 6

AFC Division: Buffalo Bills 44, Miami Dolphins 34

AFC Division: Los Angeles Raiders 20, Cincinnati Bengals 10

NFC Division: Washington Redskins 28, San Francisco 49ers 10

NFC Division: New York Giants 31, Chicago Bears 3

AFC Conference Championship: Buffalo Bills 51, Los Angeles Raiders 3

NFC Conference Championship: New York Giants 15, San Francisco 49ers 13

Super Bowl XXV: New York Giants 20, Buffalo Bills 19

## *1991*

AFC Wild Card: Kansas City Chiefs 10, Los Angeles Raiders 6

AFC Wild Card: Houston Oilers 17, New York Jets 10

NFC Wild Card: Dallas Cowboys 17, Chicago Bears 13

NFC Wild Card: Atlanta Falcons 27, New Orleans Saints 20

AFC Division: Buffalo Bills 37, Kansas City Chiefs 14

AFC Division: Denver Broncos 26, Houston Oilers 24

NFC Division: Washington Redskins 24, Atlanta Falcons 7

NFC Division: Detroit Lions 38, Dallas Cowboys 6

AFC Conference Championship: Buffalo Bills 10, Denver Broncos 7

NFC Conference Championship: Washington Redskins 41, Detroit Lions 10

Super Bowl XXVI: Washington Redskins 37, Buffalo Bills 24

# 1992

AFC Wild Card: Buffalo Bills 41, Houston Oilers 38 (OT)
AFC Wild Card: San Diego Chargers 17, Kansas City Chiefs 0
NFC Wild Card: Washington Redskins 24, Minnesota Vikings 7
NFC Wild Card: Philadelphia Eagles 36, New Orleans Saints 20
AFC Division: Buffalo Bills 24, Pittsburgh Steelers 3
AFC Division: Miami Dolphins 31, San Diego Chargers 0
NFC Division: San Francisco 49ers 20, Washington Redskins 13
NFC Division: Dallas Cowboys 34, Philadelphia Eagles 10
AFC Conference Championship: Buffalo Bills29, Miami Dolphins 10
NFC Conference Championship: Dallas Cowboys 30, San Francisco 49ers 20
Super Bowl XXVII: Dallas Cowboys 52, Buffalo Bills 17

---

### THE RECORDS

Emmitt Smith rushed for 164 touchdowns (five over the course of
three Super Bowls) and gained 18,355 yards during his career,
all more than any other player in the history of the NFL.

---

# 1993

AFC Wild Card: Los Angeles Raiders 42, Denver Broncos 24
AFC Wild Card: Kansas City Chiefs 27, Pittsburgh Steelers 24 (OT)
NFC Wild Card: New York Giants 17, Minnesota Vikings 10
NFC Wild Card: Green Bay Packers 28, Detroit Lions 24
AFC Division: Buffalo Bills 29, Los Angeles Raiders 23
AFC Division: Kansas City Chiefs 28, Houston Oilers 20
NFC Division: San Francisco 49ers 44, New York Giants 3
NFC Division: Dallas Cowboys 27, Green Bay Packers 17
AFC Conference Championship: Buffalo Bills 30, Kansas City Chiefs 13
NFC Conference Championship: Dallas Cowboys 38, San Francisco 49ers 21
Super Bowl XXVIII: Dallas Cowboys 30, Buffalo Bills 13

# EMMITT SMITH

Emmitt Smith, the 1990 Offensive Rookie of the Year and first-round pick of the Dallas Cowboys, hit the ground running, racking up 937 yards and 11 touchdowns in his NFL debut season. The following year he led the league with 1,563 rushing yards, as he did over three of the next four seasons, also leading the league in touchdowns in 1992, 1994, and 1995, and yards from scrimmage in 1993 and 1995.

In 1993, Smith was named NFL MVP and Super Bowl MVP, earning the latter after rushing for 132 yards with two touchdowns against the Bills. Emmitt Smith passed Walter Payton with more career rushing yards than any player in NFL history, retiring with 18,355. He also has more career rushing touchdowns than any other running back, at 164. He is second all-time on the career touchdown list behind only Jerry Rice.

## THE RECORDS

Charles Haley has a collection of Super Bowl rings, having played on five championship teams—more than any other player (two with San Francisco and three with Dallas). He also has more career Super Bowl sacks (4.5) than any other player since the league began compiling sack stats in 1982.

# 1994

AFC Wild Card: Cleveland Browns 20, New England Patriots 13

AFC Wild Card: Miami Dolphins 27, Kansas City Chiefs 17

NFC Wild Card: Chicago Bears 35, Minnesota Vikings 18

NFC Wild Card: Green Bay Packers 16, Detroit Lions 12

AFC Division: Pittsburgh Steelers 29, Cleveland Browns 9

AFC Division: San Diego Chargers 22, Miami Dolphins 21

NFC Division: San Francisco 49ers 44, Chicago Bears 15

NFC Division: Dallas Cowboys 35, Green Bay Packers 9

AFC Conference Championship:

San Diego Chargers 17, Pittsburgh Steelers 13

NFC Conference Championship:

San Francisco 49ers 38, Dallas Cowboys 28

Super Bowl XXIX: San Francisco 49ers 49, San Diego Chargers 26

---

## THE RECORDS

Jerry Rice has more consecutive games with a touchdown catch (13) and more Super Bowl touchdowns/points scored in Super Bowl games (8 TDs for 48 points over four games) than any other player.

# JERRY RICE

The 1985 first-round pick of the San Francisco 49ers, Jerry Rice is regarded by many as one of the greatest players in the history of the game. The list of career records he left behind, many still standing, is staggering. In his second pro season he set an NFL record with 22 touchdown receptions. Two years later he was a Super Bowl MVP in the first of four Super Bowls played across his 20-year career, three of which produced titles for the San Francisco 49ers.

A 13-time Pro Bowler, Rice left the game first all-time in touchdowns with 208, receptions with 1,549, receiving yards with 22,895, receiving touchdowns with 197, yards from scrimmage with 23,540, and all-purpose yards with 23,546. He also played and started in more playoff games than any other player to date.

## 1995

AFC Wild Card: Buffalo Bills 37, Miami Dolphins 22

AFC Wild Card: Indianapolis Colts 35, San Diego Chargers 20

NFC Wild Card: Philadelphia Eagles 58, Detroit Lions 37

NFC Wild Card: Green Bay Packers 37, Atlanta Falcons 20

AFC Division: Pittsburgh Steelers 40, Buffalo Bills 21

AFC Division: Indianapolis Colts 10, Kansas City Chiefs 7

NFC Division: Green Bay Packers 27, San Francisco 49ers 17

NFC Division: Dallas Cowboys 30, Philadelphia Eagles 11

AFC Conference Championship:
Pittsburgh Steelers 20, Indianapolis Colts 16

NFC Conference Championship:
Dallas Cowboys 38, Green Bay Packers 27
Super Bowl XXX: Dallas Cowboys 27, Pittsburgh Steelers 17

## *1996*

AFC Wild Card: Jacksonville Jaguars 30, Buffalo Bills 27
AFC Wild Card: Pittsburgh Steelers 42, Indianapolis Colts 14
NFC Wild Card: Dallas Cowboys 40, Minnesota Vikings 15
NFC Wild Card: San Francisco 49ers 14, Philadelphia Eagles 0
AFC Division: Jacksonville Jaguars 30, Denver Broncos 27
AFC Division: New England Patriots 28, Pittsburgh Steelers 3
NFC Division: Green Bay Packers 35, San Francisco 49ers 14
NFC Division: Carolina Panthers 26, Dallas Cowboys 17
AFC Conference Championship:
New England Patriots 20, Jacksonville Jaguars 6
NFC Conference Championship:
Green Bay Packers 30, Carolina Panthers 13
Super Bowl XXXI: Green Bay Packers 35, New England Patriots 21

---

### THE RECORDS

Brett Favre passed for more yards (71,838) and threw for more touchdowns (508) than any other player. He also has the record for most career games with four or more touchdown passes (23).

---

## *1997*

AFC Wild Card: Denver Broncos 42, Jacksonville Jaguars 17

AFC Wild Card: New England Patriots 17, Miami Dolphins 3

NFC Wild Card: Minnesota Vikings 23, New York Giants 22

NFC Wild Card: Tampa Bay Buccaneers 20, Detroit Lions 10

AFC Division: Denver Broncos 14, Kansas City Chiefs 10

AFC Division: Pittsburgh Steelers 7, New England Patriots 6

NFC Division: Green Bay Packers 21, Tampa Bay Buccaneers 7

NFC Division: San Francisco 49ers 38, Minnesota Vikings 22

AFC Conference Championship: Denver Broncos 24, Pittsburgh Steelers 21

NFC Conference Championship:
Green Bay Packers 23, San Francisco 49ers 10

Super Bowl XXXII: Denver Broncos 31, Green Bay Packers 24

## *1998*

AFC Wild Card: Miami Dolphins 24, Buffalo Bills 17

AFC Wild Card: Jacksonville Jaguars 25, New England Patriots 10

NFC Wild Card: Arizona Cardinals 20, Dallas Cowboys 7

NFC Wild Card: San Francisco 49ers 30, Green Bay Packers 27

AFC Division: Denver Broncos 38, Miami Dolphins 3

AFC Division: New York Jets 34, Jacksonville Jaguars 24

NFC Division: Minnesota Vikings 41, Arizona Cardinals 21

NFC Division: Atlanta Falcons 20, San Francisco 49ers 18

AFC Conference Championship: Denver Broncos 23, New York Jets 10

NFC Conference Championship:
Atlanta Falcons 30, Minnesota Vikings 27 (OT)

Super Bowl XXXIII: Denver Broncos 34, Atlanta Falcons 19

## 1999

AFC Wild Card: Tennessee Titans 22, Buffalo Bills 16

AFC Wild Card: Miami Dolphins 20, Seattle Seahawks 17

NFC Wild Card: Washington Redskins 27, Detroit Lions 13

NFC Wild Card: Minnesota Vikings 27, Dallas Cowboys 10

AFC Division: Tennessee Titans 19, Indianapolis Colts 16

AFC Division: Jacksonville Jaguars 62, Miami Dolphins 7

NFC Division: Tampa Bay Buccaneers 14, Washington Redskins 13

NFC Division: St. Louis Rams 49, Minnesota Vikings 37

AFC Conference Championship: Tennessee Titans 33, Jacksonville Jaguars 14

NFC Conference Championship:
St. Louis Rams 11, Tampa Bay Buccaneers 6

Super Bowl XXXIV: St. Louis Rams 23, Tennessee Titans 16

## 2000

AFC Wild Card: Baltimore Ravens 21, Denver Broncos 3

AFC Wild Card: Miami Dolphins 23, Indianapolis Colts 17 (OT)

NFC Wild Card: New Orleans Saints 31, St. Louis Rams 28

NFC Wild Card: Philadelphia Eagles 21, Tampa Bay Buccaneers 3

AFC Division: Baltimore Ravens 24, Tennessee Titans 10

AFC Division: Oakland Raiders 27, Miami Dolphins 0

NFC Division: New York Giants 20, Philadelphia Eagles 10

NFC Division: Minnesota Vikings 34, New Orleans Saints 16

AFC Conference Championship: Baltimore Ravens 16, Oakland Raiders 3

NFC Conference Championship: New York Giants 41, Minnesota Vikings 0

Super Bowl XXXV: Baltimore Ravens 34, New York Giants 7

## *2001*

AFC Wild Card: Baltimore Ravens 20, Miami Dolphins 3

AFC Wild Card: Oakland Raiders 38, New York Jets 24

NFC Wild Card: Green Bay Packers 25, San Francisco 49ers 15

NFC Wild Card: Philadelphia Eagles 31, Tampa Bay Buccaneers 9

AFC Division: Pittsburgh Steelers 27, Baltimore Ravens 10

AFC Division: New England Patriots 16, Oakland Raiders 13 (OT)

NFC Division: Philadelphia Eagles 33, Chicago Bears 19

NFC Division: St. Louis Rams 45, Green Bay Packers 17

AFC Conference Championship:

New England Patriots 24, Pittsburgh Steelers 17

NFC Conference Championship: St. Louis Rams 29, Philadelphia Eagles 24

Super Bowl XXXVI: New England Patriots 20, St. Louis Rams 17

---

### THE RECORDS

Adam Vinatieri has kicked more field goals in a Super Bowl than
any other player, with seven over five games (New England Patriots,
Indianapolis Colts).

---

## *2002*

AFC Wild Card: Pittsburgh Steelers 36, Cleveland Browns 33

AFC Wild Card: New York Jets 41, Indianapolis Colts 0

NFC Wild Card: San Francisco 49ers 39, New York Giants 38

NFC Wild Card: Atlanta Falcons 27, Green Bay Packers 7

AFC Division: Oakland Raiders 30, New York Jets 10

AFC Division: Tennessee Titans 34, Pittsburgh Steelers 31 (OT)

NFC Division: Philadelphia Eagles 20, Atlanta Falcons 6

NFC Division: Tampa Bay Buccaneers 31, San Francisco 49ers 6
AFC Conference Championship: Oakland Raiders 41, Tennessee Titans 24
NFC Conference Championship:
Tampa Bay Buccaneers 27, Philadelphia Eagles 10
Super Bowl XXXVII: Tampa Bay Buccaneers 48, Oakland Raiders 21

## *2003*

AFC Wild Card: Tennessee Titans 20, Baltimore Ravens 17
AFC Wild Card: Indianapolis Colts 41, Denver Broncos 10
NFC Wild Card: Green Bay Packers 33, Seattle Seahawks 27 (OT)
NFC Wild Card: Carolina Panthers 29, Dallas Cowboys 10
AFC Division: Indianapolis Colts 38, Kansas City Chiefs 31
AFC Division: New England Patriots 17, Tennessee Titans 14
NFC Division: Carolina Panthers 29, St. Louis Rams 23 (OT)
NFC Division: Philadelphia Eagles 20, Green Bay Packers 17 (OT)
AFC Conference Championship: New England Patriots 24, Indianapolis Colts 14
NFC Conference Championship: Carolina Panthers 14, Philadelphia Eagles 3
Super Bowl XXXVIII: New England Patriots 32, Carolina Panthers 29

## *2004*

AFC Wild Card: Indianapolis Colts 49, Denver Broncos 24
AFC Wild Card: New York Jets 20, San Diego Chargers 17 (OT)
NFC Wild Card: Minnesota Vikings 31, Green Bay Packers 17

---

### THE RECORDS

Jake Delhomme threw the longest completed pass in Super Bowl history,
an 85-yard touchdown to Muhsin Muhammad in Super Bowl XXXVIII.

---

NFC Wild Card: St. Louis Rams 27, Seattle Seahawks 20

AFC Division: New England Patriots 20, Indianapolis Colts 3

AFC Division: Pittsburgh Steelers 20, New York Jets 17 (OT)

NFC Division: Atlanta Falcons 47, St. Louis Rams 17

NFC Division: Philadelphia Eagles 27, Minnesota Vikings 14

AFC Conference Championship:

New England Patriots 41, Pittsburgh Steelers 27

NFC Conference Championship: Philadelphia Eagles 27, Atlanta Falcons 10

Super Bowl XXXIX: New England Patriots 24, Philadelphia Eagles 21

## *2005*

AFC Wild Card: Pittsburgh Steelers 31, Cincinnati Bengals 17

AFC Wild Card: New England Patriots 28, Jacksonville Jaguars 3

NFC Wild Card: Washington Redskins 17, Tampa Bay Buccaneers 10

NFC Wild Card: Carolina Panthers 23, New York Giants 0

AFC Division: Denver Broncos 27, New England Patriots 13

AFC Division: Pittsburgh Steelers 21, Indianapolis Colts 18

NFC Division: Seattle Seahawks 20, Washington Redskins 10

NFC Division: Carolina Panthers 29, Chicago Bears 21

AFC Conference Championship: Pittsburgh Steelers 34, Denver Broncos 17

NFC Conference Championship: Seattle Seahawks 34, Carolina Panthers 14

Super Bowl XL: Pittsburgh Steelers 21, Seattle Seahawks 10

## *2006*

AFC Wild Card: Indianapolis Colts 23, Kansas City Chiefs 8

AFC Wild Card: New England Patriots 37, New York Jets 16

NFC Wild Card: Philadelphia Eagles 23, New York Giants 20

NFC Wild Card: Seattle Seahawks 21, Dallas Cowboys 20

AFC Division: Indianapolis Colts 15, Baltimore Ravens 6

AFC Division: New England Patriots 24, San Diego Chargers 21

NFC Division: Chicago Bears 27, Seattle Seahawks 24 (OT)

NFC Division: New Orleans Saints 27, Philadelphia Eagles 24

AFC Conference Championship:
Indianapolis Colts 38, New England Patriots 34

NFC Conference Championship: Chicago Bears 39, New Orleans Saints 14

Super Bowl XLI: Indianapolis Colts 29, Chicago Bears 17

---

### THE RECORDS

Devin Hester of the Chicago Bears has the career record for touchdowns
scored on punt returns (12).

---

## *2007*

AFC Wild Card: Jacksonville Jaguars 31, Pittsburgh Steelers 29

AFC Wild Card: San Diego Chargers 17, Tennessee Titans 6

NFC Wild Card: Seattle Seahawks 35, Washington Redskins 14

NFC Wild Card: New York Giants 24, Tampa Bay Buccaneers 14

AFC Division: San Diego Chargers 28, Indianapolis Colts 24

AFC Division: New England Patriots 31, Jacksonville Jaguars 20

NFC Division: New York Giants 21, Dallas Cowboys 17

NFC Division: Green Bay Packers 42, Seattle Seahawks 20

AFC Conference Championship:
New England Patriots 21, San Diego Chargers 12

NFC Conference Championship: New York Giants 23, Green Bay Packers 20 (OT)

Super Bowl XLII: New York Giants 17, New England Patriots 14

## THE RECORDS

The 2007 New England Patriots went 16-0 in the regular season—the only undefeated 16-game season in the history of the game. New England also scored 75 touchdowns that year—the most by a team in a single season. The Pats' quest for a perfect 19-0 run in 2007 would be denied in the final minutes of Super Bowl XLII by the New York Giants.

## *2008*

AFC Wild Card: Baltimore Ravens 27, Miami Dolphins 9

AFC Wild Card: San Diego Chargers 23, Indianapolis Colts 17 (OT)

NFC Wild Card: Arizona Cardinals 30, Atlanta Falcons 24

NFC Wild Card: Philadelphia Eagles 26, Minnesota Vikings 14

AFC Division: Baltimore Ravens 13, Tennessee Titans 10

AFC Division: Pittsburgh Steelers 35, San Diego Chargers 24

NFC Division: Philadelphia Eagles 23, New York Giants 11

NFC Division: Arizona Cardinals 33, Carolina Panthers 13

AFC Conference Championship: Pittsburgh Steelers 23, Baltimore Ravens 14

NFC Conference Championship: Arizona Cardinals 32, Philadelphia Eagles 25

Super Bowl XLIII: Pittsburgh Steelers 27, Arizona Cardinals 23

## *2009*

AFC Wild Card: Baltimore Ravens 33, New England Patriots 14

AFC Wild Card: New York Jets 24, Cincinnati Bengals 14

NFC Wild Card: Arizona Cardinals 51, Green Bay Packers 45 (OT)

NFC Wild Card: Dallas Cowboys 34, Philadelphia Eagles 14

AFC Division: Indianapolis Colts 20, Baltimore Ravens 3

AFC Division: New York Jets 17, San Diego Chargers 14

NFC Division: New Orleans Saints 45, Arizona Cardinals 14
NFC Division: Minnesota Vikings 34, Dallas Cowboys 3
AFC Conference Championship: Indianapolis Colts 30, New York Jets 17
NFC Conference Championship:
New Orleans Saints 31, Minnesota Vikings 28 (OT)
Super Bowl XLIV: New Orleans Saints 31, Indianapolis Colts 17

---

## THE RECORDS

Drew Brees of the New Orleans Saints and Peyton Manning of the
Indianapolis Colts met in Super Bowl XLIV. The following season Manning
completed 450 passes and Brees completed 448, with backup quarterback
Chase Daniel completing two more. At 450 each, both
teams share the single-season mark for most completed passes.

---

## *2010*

AFC Wild Card: Baltimore Ravens 30, Kansas City Chiefs 7
AFC Wild Card: New York Jets 17, Indianapolis Colts 16
NFC Wild Card: Green Bay Packers 21, Philadelphia Eagles 16
NFC Wild Card: Seattle Seahawks 41, New Orleans Saints 36
AFC Division: Pittsburgh Steelers 31, Baltimore Ravens 24
AFC Division: New York Jets 28, New England Patriots 21
NFC Division: Chicago Bears 35, Seattle Seahawks 24
NFC Division: Green Bay Packers 48, Atlanta Falcons 21
AFC Conference Championship: Pittsburgh Steelers 24, New York Jets 19
NFC Conference Championship: Green Bay Packers 21, Chicago Bears 14
Super Bowl XLV: Green Bay Packers 31, Pittsburgh Steelers 25

# Appendix

*In writing this book, it was only my intention to present an accessible history of the game that gathered up some of what I found to be its more interesting items of trivia. In researching that history, there was a reoccurring theme that I couldn't help but notice. In every sense and on every level, football is a game of change that thrives when it adapts to changes made around it. While baseball holds on to its traditions for dear life and hasn't had a major change to how the game is played since the mound was lowered in 1969 and the DH was added in 1973, football is constantly in motion. Whether it's the two-point conversion, the overtime rules, or the spot of the kickoff, the game continues to look at itself and make adjustments.*

*With the changing nature of the game in mind, I present three passages from Walter Camp, the father of modern football. Camp's nineteenth-century book,* American Football, *was a primer on the game for players, coaches, and fans alike. I feature them here because they not only expand upon topics discussed earlier in this book, but also because throughout each of them you can see examples of how far the game has come from its origins.*

Historic images like this one are reminders of how much
the game of football has evolved over the years

# *American Football*

## *by Walter Camp (1891)*

## ENGLISH AND AMERICAN RUGBY

Rugby football—for it is from the Rugby Union Rules that our American Intercollegiate game was derived—dates its present era of popularity from formation in England, in 1871, of a union of some score of clubs. Nearly 10 years before this there had been an attempt made to unite the various diverging football factions under a common set of laws; but this proved a failure, and the styles of play became farther and farther apart. Of the Association game one can say but little as regards its American following. It is quite extensively played in this country, but more by those who have themselves played it in Great Britain than by native-born Americans. Its popularity is extending, and at some day it will very likely become as well understood in this country as the derived Rugby is to-day. Its essential characteristic is, that it is played with the feet, in distinction from the Rugby, in which the ball may be carried in the hands.

To revert to the Rugby Union. Years before the formation of this association the game was played by sides almost unlimited in numbers.

One of the favorite school matches was "Sixth form against all the rest of the school." Twenty on a side, however, became the ruling number; but this was, after a time, replaced by fifteens, as the days of twenties proved only shoving matches. With the reduction in numbers came increased running and an added interest. This change to fifteens was made in 1877, at the request of Scotland. At once there followed a more open style of play, and before long short passing became common. In 1882 the Oxford team instituted the long low pass to the open, and by the use of it remained undefeated for three seasons.

After the decrease to fifteen men the number of three-quarter-backs, who really represent our American half-backs, was increased from one to two, and two full-backs were played. A little later British captains put another full-back up into the three-quarter line, playing only one full-back.

The Englishmen also play two men whom they call half-backs, but whose duties are like those of our quarter-backs, for they seize the ball when it comes out of the scrimmage and pass it to a three-quarter for a run.

Nine men is the usual number for an English rush line, although a captain will sometimes take his ninth rusher back as a fourth three-quarter-back. There is much discussion as to when this should be done. The captain selects his men much as we do in America, and he is generally himself a player of some position behind the line, centre three-quarter being preferred. The opening play in an English Rugby game is, as a rule, a high kick well followed up. If one will bear in mind that the half backs are, like our quarter, the ones to seize the ball when it emerges from a scrimmage and pass it to the three-quarters, he will gain some idea of the character of the English method. He should understand, however, that the English half-back is obliged to look out sharply for the ball, because it comes out by chance and at random, and not directly as in our game, when the quarter can usually expect to receive the ball without trouble from the snap-back.

The forwards in an English match endeavor, when a scrimmage occurs, by kicking and pushing to drive the ball in the direction of their opponents' goal line, and they become extremely expert in the use of their feet. There are two umpires, whose duty it is to make claims (which they do by raising their flags), and a referee, who allows or disallows these claims. The penalty for fouls, which was at first only a down, is now in many cases a free kick.

The American game, it must be remembered, came from Rugby Union in 1875, and not from the Rugby Union of to-day, although the changes in the English game have been by no manner of means commensurate with those made on this side the water. Being bound by no traditions, and having seen no play, the American took the English rules for a starting-point, and almost immediately proceeded to add and subtract, according to what seemed his pressing needs. And they were many. A favored few, whose intercourse with Canadian players had given them some of the English ideas, were able to explain the knotty points to a small degree, but not enough to really assist the mass of uninitiated players to an under-standing. Misinterpretations were so numerous as to render satisfactory rulings almost out of the question and explanatory legislation imperative. In the autumn of 1876 the first game under Rugby rules between American colleges was played at New Haven, and before another was attempted a convention had tried its hand at correcting the weak points, as they appeared to the minds of the legislators, in the Rugby Union Rules.

The feature of the American game in distinction from the English is, just as it was within a year from the time of the adoption of the sport, the *outlet of the scrimmage.*

In this lies the backbone to which the entire body of American football is attached. The English half-backs stand outside the scrimmage, and when the ball pops out it is their duty to seize it and pass it out to a three-quarter, who runs with it. The American quarter-back stands behind the scrimmage and gives a signal, immediately after which he knows the ball will come directly into his hands to be passed for a run or a kick. What is, therefore, in the English game a matter of considerable chance is "cut-and-dried" in the American game; and the element of chance being eliminated, opportunity is given for the display in the latter fame of far more skill in the development of brilliant plays and carefully planned manoeuvres.

The Americans started with the English scrimmage, kicked at the ball, and pushed and scrambled for a season, until it was discovered that a very clever manifestation of the play was to let the opponents do the kicking— in fact, to leave an opening at the proper moment through which the ball would come, and a man a few feet behind this opening could always get the ball and pass it while the men who kicked it were still entangled in the scrimmage. After a little of this, no one was anxious to kick the ball through, and the rushers began to roll the ball sidewise along between the lines. Then almost immediately it was discovered that a man could snap the ball backwards with his toe, and the American outlet was installed.

At first the play was crude in the extreme, but even in its earliest stages it proved distinctly more satisfactory to both player and spectator than the kicking and shoving which marked the English method.

The same man did not always snap the ball back as he does now, but any one of the rushers would do it upon occasion. The men did not preserve their relative positions in the line, and any one of the men behind the line would act as a quarter-back. Such a condition of affairs could not, however, last long where intercollegiate rivalry proved such an incentive to the perfection of play, and the positions of centre-rush or snap-back and quarter-back became the most distinctive of any upon the field. The centre-rush at that time was selected more for his agility, strange to say, than for his weight and strength; but in case he was a light man he was always flanked by two heavy guards. One season's play convinced all captains that the centre selection of the forward line must be heavy, and if any light-weights were to be used among the rushers they should be near the wings.

Quarter-back has, from the very outset, been a position in which a small man can be used to great advantage. The half-backs and backs have usually been men of speed coupled with skill as kickers.

The number originally adopted for matches in this country was eleven on a side. From some silly notion that it would increase the skill displayed, this number was changed to fifteen, although the Englishmen were moving in the other direction by reducing their numbers from twenties to fifteens. A year or two of fifteen on a side drove the American players back to elevens, and there the number has rested.

In the early days of the sport, while the players individually were courageous, the team play was cowardly; that is, the tacticians were so taken up with a study of defence—how to protect the goal—that the attack was weak. The direct result of this was to place too few men in the forward line and too many behind it. If to-day we were to revert to fifteen on a side, there is little doubt that we should throw eleven of them up into the rush line, and upon occasion even twelve. We now realize that the best defence does not consist in planning how to stop a man after he has obtained a fair start towards the goal, but in throwing all available force up against him before he can get free of the forward line. The only way to effectively defeat this aggressive defence is by means of skilled kicking. It is possible with really good kickers to throw a team playing in this fashion into disorder by well-laced and long punting, followed up most sharply; but it requires nerve and an unfailing accuracy of aim and judgment.

It is only a few years ago that it required considerable argument to convince a captain that he could with safety send one of his halves up into the forward line when his opponents had the ball; but it will take better kicking than is exhibited in most of the championship matches to frighten that halfback out of the line now. Even the quarter was wont upon occasion to drop back among the halves and assist them rather than the rushers.

All the tendency for the last two years has been towards diminishing the number of men held in reserve, as it were, behind the line, and increasing by this means the crushing force by which the forwards might check either runner or kicker before his play could be executed.

Should the English ever adopt an outlet for their scrimmage, making the play as direct as is ours, their men would gravitate to the forward line as rapidly as have our players.

Next to the difference in scrimmage outlet between our game and that of the British stands a much more recent development, which we call interference. This is the assistance given to a runner by a companion or companions who go before him and break a path for him or shoulder off would-be tacklers. This, to the Englishman, would be the most detestable kind of off-side play, and not tolerated for an instant upon any field in the United Kingdom.

Even into this the Americans did not plunge suddenly, but rather little by little they stepped in, until it was necessary to do one of two things—either legalize what was being tacitly consented to, or penalize it heavily. The result was that it was legalized. With this concession, though, there went a certain condition which gained a measure of confidence for the new ruling.

To understand just how this state of affairs above mentioned came about one should know that, in the attempt to block opponents when the quarter-back was receiving and passing the ball, the forwards fell into the habit of extending their arms horizontally from the shoulder, as by this method each man could cover more space. For a number of years this went on without detriment to the sport in any way, but after a time there was more or less complaint of holding in the line, and it was ruled that a man must not change his position after the ball was snapped, nor bend his arms about an opponent at such a time. Unfortunately the referee (for at this stage of the game there was no umpire) could not watch the ball and the players with sufficient care to enforce this ruling, and the temper of the players suffered accordingly. It is always the case when a rule is not enforced unflinchingly, no matter from what cause, that both sides suffer, and the tendency always is towards devising additional infringements. The additional infringement in this instance was even worse than could have been foreseen; for, not content with simply blocking or even holding an opponent until the quarter should have passed the ball in safety, the players in the forward line saw an opportunity for going a step farther, and actually began the practice of seizing an opponent long after the ball had been played, and dragging him out of the way of the running half-back. In the thick of the rush line this was frequently possible without risk of discovery by the referee; and, emboldened by successes of this kind, men would reach out even in the open, and drag back a struggling tackier just as he was about to lay his hands upon the runner. It was this state of affairs which brought up the question, "How much should a comrade be allowed to aid the runner?"

American football legislators answered this question satisfactorily, after long discussion, by determining that the runner might be assisted to any extent, provided the assistant did not use his hands or arms in performing this office. The first result of this was to lower the arms of the rushers when lined up, and, in spite of some forebodings, this proved really a benefit to the game. The second result has been to perfect a system of flanking a runner by companions who form almost an impassable barrier at times to the would-be tacklers.

At the same time with mention of the solution of this problem, one should also call attention to a menace which threatened American football far more seriously than did this; and that, too, at a time when the sport was by no means so strong in years or popularity as when this later difficulty arose. I refer to the "block game." This method of play, which consisted in a succession of "downs" without advance and without allowing the opponents any chance of securing possession of the ball, proved a means by which a weak team could avoid defeat. The whole object of the match was thus frustrated, the game resulting in no score.

To meet this difficulty a rule was introduced making it incumbent upon a side to advance the ball five yards or retreat with it ten in three "downs." If this advance or retreat were not accomplished, the ball went at once into the possession of the opponents. Never did a rule in any sport work so immediate and satisfactory a reform as did this five-yard rule.

Within the last few years there has been no important change in the conduct of the American game, nor in the rules. Outside of the above-mentioned points of difference between it and the English game, there is only that of the methods of enforcing rules and determining differences. The English have a referee and two umpires, although the umpires are sometimes replaced by touch judges. The umpires act, as did the judges in our game of ten years ago, as advocates for their respective sides, and it is this advocacy which is causing them to fall into disfavor there exactly as they did here. Touch-judges merely watch the lines of the field, and decide when and where the ball goes into touch. In cases where they are employed, the referee renders all decisions upon claim of the captains. In our method there is a division of labor, but along different lines. Our two officials, the umpire and referee, have their separate provinces, the former ruling upon the conduct of players as to off-side and other offences, while the latter determines questions of fact as to when the ball is held or goes into touch, also whether a goal is kicked or not. As the rule has it, the umpire is judge for the players, and the referee for the ball.

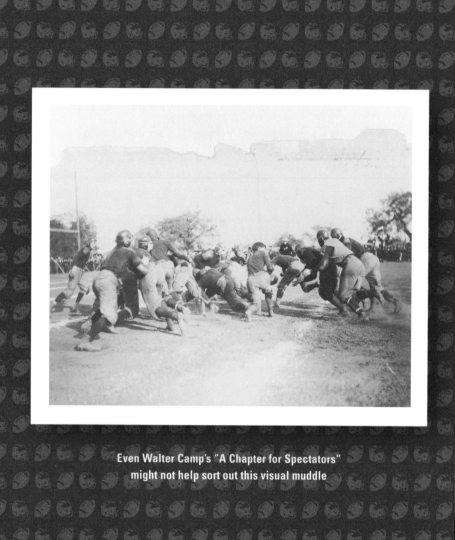

Even Walter Camp's "A Chapter for Spectators"
might not help sort out this visual muddle

# A CHAPTER FOR SPECTATORS

To those who have never played the game of football, but who chance to open the covers of this book, a short explanation of the divisions and duties of the players will not be out of place. For these this chapter is added.

The game is played by two teams, of eleven men each, upon a field 330 feet long and 160 feet wide, at either end of which are goal-posts with a cross-bar.

The ball, which is like a large leather egg, is placed in the centre of this field, and each team endeavors to drive it in the direction of the opponents' goal-line, where any scoring must be done. Goals and touch-downs are the only points which count, and these can be made only as follows:

A goal can be obtained by kicking the ball in any way except a punt (a certain kind of kick where the ball is dropped by a player and kicked before touching the ground) over the cross-bar of the opponents' goal. A touch-down is obtained by touching the ball to the ground behind the line of the goal. So, in either case, the ball must cross the end of the field in some way to make any score. The sole object, then, of all the struggles which take place in the field is to advance the ball to a position such that scoring is possible. A firm grasp of this idea usually simplifies matters very much for the casual spectator.

The object of the white lines which cross the field at every five yards is merely to assist the referee in determining how far the ball moves at a time; for there is a rule which states that a team must advance the ball five yards in three attempts or retreat with it twenty. If they do not succeed in doing this, the other side takes possession of the ball, and in their turn try to advance it.

There are certain rules which govern the methods of making these advances, any infringement of which constitutes what is called *a foul*, and entails a penalty upon the side making it.

Any player can run with the ball or kick it if, when he receives it, he is "on side"—that is, between the ball and his own goal-line. He may not take the ball if he is "off side"— that is, between the ball and his opponents' goal-line— until an adversary has touched the ball.

Whenever a player running with the ball is held, he must cry "down," and a man of his side then places the ball on the ground and snaps it back. This puts it in play, and is called a scrimmage, and this scrimmage is the most commonly recurring feature of the game.

For the purposes of advancing the ball or repelling the attack of the opponents it has proved advisable for a captain to divide his eleven men into two general divisions: the forwards and backs. The forwards, of whom there are seven, are usually called rushers, and they make practically a straight line across the field when the ball is put in play on a "down." Next behind them is the quarter-back, who does the passing of the ball to one or another of the players, while just behind him are the two half-backs and the back, usually in something of a triangle in arrangement, with the last named nearest the goal which his team is defending.

The following definitions will also aid the spectator in understanding many of the expressions used by the devotees of the sport:

A *drop-kick* is made by letting the ball fall from the hands, and kicking it at the very instant it rises.

A *place-kick* is made by kicking the ball after it has been placed on the ground.

A *punt* is made by letting the ball fall from the hands, and kicking it before it touches the ground.

*Kick-off* is a place-kick from the centre of the field of play.

*Kick-out* is a drop-kick, or place-kick, by a player of the side which has touched the ball down in their own goal, or into whose touch-in-goal the ball has gone.

*In touch* means out of bounds.

*A fair* is putting the ball in play, from touch.

A *foul* is any violation of a rule.

A *touch-down* is made when the ball is carried, kicked, or passed across the goal-line and there held, either in goal or touch-in-goal.

A *safety* is made when a player, guarding his goal, receives the ball from a player of his own side, and touches it down behind his goal-line, or carries the ball across his own goal-line and touches it down, or puts the ball into his own touch-in-goal.

A *touch-back* is made when a player touches the ball to the ground behind his own goal, the impetus which sent the ball across the line having been received from an opponent.

A *fair catch* is a catch made direct from a kick by one of the opponents, provided the catcher made a mark with his heel at the spot where he made the catch.

*Interference* is using the hands or arms in any way to obstruct or hold a player who has got the ball.

The *penalty* for fouls and violation of rules, except otherwise provided, is a down for the other side; or, if the side making the foul has not the ball, five yards to the opponents.

The following is the value of each point in the scoring:

Goal obtained by touch-down, 6. Goal from field kick, 5. Touch-down failing goal, 4. Safety by opponents, 2.

The rules which bear most directly upon the play are:

The time of a game is an hour and a half, each side playing forty-five minutes from each goal. There is ten minutes' intermission between the two halves, and the game is decided by the score of even halves.

The ball is kicked off at the beginning of each half; and whenever a goal has been obtained, the side which has lost it shall kick off.

A player may throw or pass the ball in any direction except towards opponents' goal. If the ball be batted or thrown forward, it shall go down on the spot to opponents.

If a player having the ball be tackled and the ball fairly held, the man so tackling shall cry "held," the one so tackled must cry "down," and some player of his side put it down for a scrimmage. If, in three consecutive fairs and downs, unless the ball cross the goal-line, a team shall not have advanced the ball five or taken it back twenty yards, it shall go to the opponents on spot of fourth.

If the ball goes into touch, whether it bounds back or not, a player on the side which touches it down must bring it to the spot where the line was crossed, and there either bound the ball in the field of play, or touch it in with both hands, at right angles to the touch-line, and then run with it, kick it, or throw it back; or throw it out at right angles to the touch-line; or walk out with it at right angles to touch-line, any distance not less than five nor more than fifteen yards, and there put it down.

A side which has made a touch-down in their opponents' goal *must* try at goal.

# THE EFFECT OF THE CHANGES
# IN RULES.

In no sport so much as football does a slight alteration in a rule effect such remarkable changes in the style of play. When, therefore, a number of essentially radical alterations are introduced and a general revision made, as has been done in 1894, there can be little doubt of our seeing some remarkable effects. Many of them will be agreeable to the spectator and probably to a considerable proportion of the players, although the older players are always conservative about any alterations in a rule. Perhaps, therefore, it is well at the outset of this chapter to state the reasons which led to this general revision.

The tendency developed in the last three or four years towards more closeness of play led to an over-reliance by the captains upon wedge and mass plays of all descriptions. This was only natural, because it was by means of these plays that possession of the ball could be most advantageously continued. Except at opening plays, these methods were not productive of long gains or brilliant runs, but partook of a general hammering nature, yielding, however, enough to make the five yards in three downs. No one could afford to ignore the fact that in close, hard-fought games, and particularly in rainy weather, these were the safest tactics to adopt. But all this meant a general disregard of the kicking game and the sacrifice of long passes and brilliant methods to something which should be safer in the captain's eye. The interest of the spectator, and especially the interest of the spectator who was fairly versed in the game, began to wane under these conditions, and there was a great deal of dissatisfaction felt even with the play of 1892. When all these faults became still more exaggerated in 1893, there was a loud call for action of some kind; and by the time the season was ended players and the public were ready for, at any rate, the first steps towards the curtailment of the close play and a reintroduction of the more open kicking methods. The University Athletic Club, at the invitation of some of the leading colleges, appointed a committee of experts, who held meetings during the winter and spring, and in May proposed a set of rules which were accepted by the University Athletic Club, and adopted to govern the Harvard-Yale contest, and later by the Intercollegiate Association.

So far for an explanation of the causes which led to the general revision. The effect upon the play no one can be sure of. The wedge and mass plays will undoubtedly still be continued, though not to so great an extent; and the kicking will surely not be, as a great many have supposed, the general feature of the contest in the future. It will take more severe legislation to bring such a change as that about. The game will, however, open with a kick, and very likely, when there is much wind, with two kicks—that is, the winner of the toss, having his choice of goal or kick-off, will probably take goal, and the opponents will, therefore, have the kick-off. The new rules provide that this kick-off must be an actual kick into the opponent's territory of, at least, ten yards, so that it is probable that we shall see the old-fashioned start once more. But the side receiving the ball, having the wind with them, will be inclined to take an early opportunity of returning the kick, so that, as stated above, we shall probably see two kicks early in the game. The running play may even be deferred until the ball has been thus kicked and returned, and the opening play, by the holder's flying wedge or an attempt made to hold the ball through a succession of downs until a touch-down is secured, will be done away with. The final difference, however, will not be very great, because after the return kick the side playing against the wind will then naturally endeavor to play a running game and hold the ball as long as possible. To sum up the first few minutes of the game, therefore, it is not unlikely that we shall see the side which started off in possession of the ball beginning their running game, instead of at the middle of the field, some ten or fifteen yards back of that centre, dependent, of course, upon the force of the wind, and beginning with a down instead of with the flying wedge.

Having gone thus far into the game, the effect of the more stringent rule against fouls will be of interest. Instead of five yards, the penalty has been increased to ten yards for fouls and violation of the rules, unless the offending side has the ball, in which case the penalty is the same as of old—that is, an immediate surrender of the ball to the opponents. This at once brings a new element into the game, because the penalty for a foul to the side holding the ball is no greater than it was a year ago, but the penalty inflicted upon the side acting on the defence is doubled. Just what the outcome of this will be is hard to say; but the first thought is that it will benefit the attack, and so, perhaps, make it easier to retain possession of the ball and make distance. It is certain that it will tend to make the captain drill his men to a very strict observation of the rules when on the defence. So far, then, we find that the captain and coach will have to educate their men for good place kicking; and by "good" is meant not only long place kicking, but a development of accuracy as well, and an even more rapid following up of the play than ever before. Then the captain must hold his men under the greatest restraint, to prevent their getting off side during the scrimmage when the opponents have the ball.

The next point we come to is that of the fair catch. Here a provision has been made that will give the catcher protection if he so desires it; but it is hardly probable that many of the men will take regular advantage of that protection—that is, instead of holding up the hand, and thus confining himself to a fair catch, the halfback or full-back will very probably not hold up his hand, but take the chance in a great many kicks of a run with the ball. Of course, when it is a high kick, or he is surrounded by his opponents, he will put up his hand and heel the ball; but he is not likely to put up his hand until the last moment, and then only when there is no chance for a run. To tell the truth, the half-back and backs are really not so afraid of being thrown as they are of muffing the ball, for all the pity which has been bestowed upon them in the past.

Apropos of these offences, the third official or linesman will be of considerable assistance to the umpire and referee on fouls as well as on timing the game. He will probably confine his work mostly to the side lines, in keeping track of the downs and distance covered. This, as well as all his other conduct, is, however, under the advice of the umpire or the referee, and he is, therefore, by no manner of means as important an official as either of these.

Fields will be kept clear by a rule which provides that only one man, and he presumably competent to take care of an injured player, shall go upon the field in case of an accident.

When the ball goes into touch we shall see no more scrimmages on the side of the field as we have at times, for the player cannot bound it in and run with it, but he must either walk out and put it down in accordance with the most common fashion, or touch it in and kick it. This latter play is seldom seen, and :fairs" will probably resolve themselves into what they have been practically for the last few years—namely, a down fifteen yards from the side line.

The effect of limiting the time of the game to an hour and ten minutes will be to make the playing faster and even more dashing than formerly, for it will be the duty of the captains to get all the play possible out of their men in the two shortened halves. Moreover, no time being allowed to recover breath will keep the play going with such continuity that spectators will hardly be bored by the slowness of the progress.

Perhaps the most important change in methods will appear when the ball goes inside the twenty-five yard line of either goal. In the case where it is in the possession of the defenders of the goal, they will strive very hard to retain possession of it, or to surrender it to the other side at some point outside of the twenty-five yard line. Where, on the other hand, it is in possession of the attacking side, if their running game is not working very well, they will likely enough resort at once to a drop kick, because by the new rule if that kick fails the opponents can bring the ball out only to the ten-yard line instead of the twenty-five-yard line. The fact is at once plain that this really means a kick out from behind one's own goal, and in addition to this it must be a kick, for the defenders of the side cannot run the ball out. This, like the rule increasing the distance for fouls, is hard on the defending side, and will probably result in more scoring than formerly.

The rule limiting mass-momentum plays is not sufficiently strong to curtail them very materially, but it will take off some of the extra weight which has been used in these plays in the past, and in that way will be of service. While only three men can get in motion before the ball is snapped, they will be joined by others who stand still until the ball is actually put in play, so that while we shall not see six or seven men at ten or fifteen yards back starting in a mass and getting under full headway before the ball is snapped, we shall undoubtedly see three men doing this, and being joined by others upon their approaching the line. The ordinary flying wedge at the opening play and on fair catches is, however, relegated to the background by the rule that the ball must be actually kicked, so that we shall see these momentum plays used only on downs.

A general survey of the situation leads one to believe that the cardinal points of the play will remain very much the same; that, in fact, the men who have thoroughly learned their positions in the past few years will be the best men for the new methods, because the new methods are only the cutting out of the exaggerated faults that have come in the last two years. Coaches will find it necessary to have on their teams not only runners but kickers, and the education of the rush line cannot be left merely to mass plays and pushing, but must consist of an intimate knowledge of the possibilities of a kicking game and the way to hold the ground gained by kicks as well as how to defend their own side. How to use the kick-off will be a very interesting problem, as will also whether to make a fair catch or not. There certainly will be times when it will be more advantageous for a man not to make a fair catch than to make it, which seems very strange. Then, too, at what particular point to try a drop kick when inside the twenty-five-yard line is likely to make plenty of study.

For the early practice and preliminary work in the game under these changed conditions a few suggestions may be serviceable.

While it will be quite practicable for a team desiring to do so to continue the running game to the absolute exclusion of any open playing, and while such a team, if well drilled and expert in their team work, will be almost as dangerous to face as ever, there has been enough of a premium placed upon kicking to make it unsafe for a team in the first class to ignore that feature. Almost the first thing to do, then, is to provide that among the candidates for the team there may be enough kicking-halves and full-backs to last through the season for both sides—the "varsity" and the "scrub." Something of a kicking game should be practised daily, to the exclusion for a time of the running play—say for fifteen or twenty minutes. A team to play a really effective kicking game must, in addition to having the punters able to place their kicks with accuracy, be equipped with a set of signals by means of which the forwards may know the direction and approximately the distance of the kick. Short kicks and putting the men on side will become again worthy of consideration. Kicking into touch will assume more of the importance it holds in the English Rugby Union. Perhaps kicking by the quarter—such as was done years ago by Mason of Harvard, and last year practised by the University of Pennsylvania team—may once more be revived. All these plays can be used in combination with the running game, but to develop them up to the level of the play will mean hard work. Still another feature of the game entailed by this kicking method will be the greater necessity for pace among the forwards. How the heavy men of our present forward lines will stand the more rapid progress up and down the field that a very lively interchange of kicks, should they take place, might mean, is a grave question. But it will never do to lighten up the line very much so long as the opponents have the right to send any crushing force of several interferers in front of the runner, for heavy men alone can stand the frequent meeting of such onslaughts.

It will be well for the captains and coaches to once again consider a more general passing game—more of the short-passing of the English player when tackled, as well as such doubles and long passes as Princeton showed the possibility of accomplishing even under the rules of 1893. A short pass for a return kick when the back, catching the ball, is not yet tackled, but too hard pressed to get in his kick, is worth a reintroduction.

For all this style of play, and one hopes its development will be considerable, life and activity are essential, and it is but fair to warn the over-zealous captains against working their men too hard. It will be even a more serious error "to take the edge off" a team before its final effort under the new rules than under the old. Work enough to develop the skill, but not enough to take the heart out of the men, will be the only way to make a first-class team. The exaggerated features of summer training will, it is to be devoutly hoped, yield to a better sense in a few years, and instead of having men tired of the play before mid-season, we shall find them as eager as ever up to the very end.

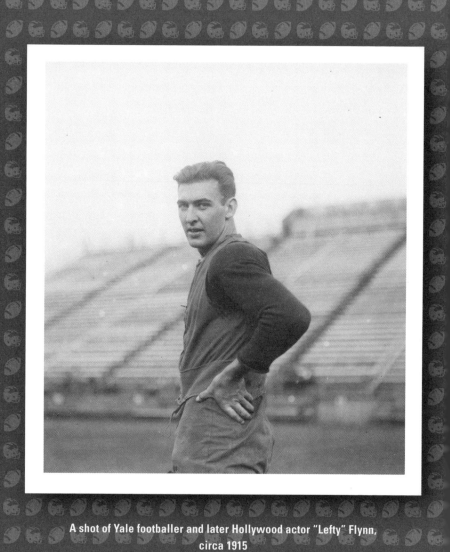

A shot of Yale footballer and later Hollywood actor "Lefty" Flynn, circa 1915

Otis Love Guernsey, shown in this 1902 shot, was a Yalie, kicker, and "squash tennis" player

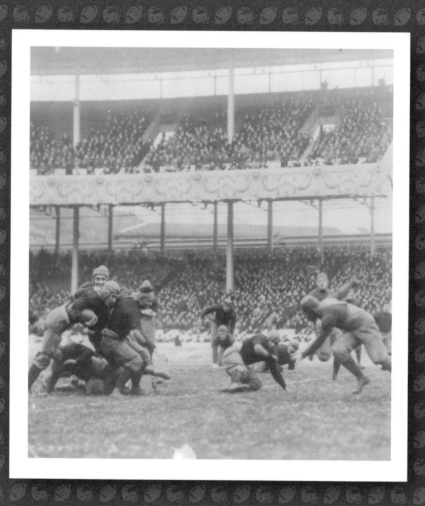

Army-Navy game at the Polo Grounds in Manhattan, 1916.
Army emerged victorious 15-7

An original football groupie, circa 1906

# ★ REFERENCES ★

"10 Key Facts About the World Cup Business—Figures," *International Business Times*, June 9, 2010.

"A Brief History of the Game: Football's Early Beginnings," www.hornetfootball.org/documents/football-history.htm.

Badenhausen, Kurt, Michael K. Ozanian, and Christina Settimi. "The Most Valuable NFL Teams," Forbes.com, August 25, 2010.

Camp, Walter. *American Football*. New York: Harper & Brothers Publishers, 1894.

"Canton Bulldogs," www.ohiohistorycentral.org/entry.php?rec=2109.

"The Case against Football," *Collier's Weekly*, Vol. 30, p. 9, March 28, 1903.

"The Christmas Truce," www.firstworldwar.com/features/christmastruce.htm.

"Close Reading: Did Grantland Rice Misquote Grantland Rice's Most Famous Quote?" http://deadspin.com/5821795/close-reading-did-grantland-rice-misquote-grantland-rices-most-famous-quote.

Davis, Jeff. *Papa Bear: The Life and Legacy of George Halas*. New York: McGraw-Hill, 2004.

Davis, Jeff. *Rozelle: Czar of the NFL*. New York: McGraw-Hill, 2007.

Gallagher, Robert. "The Galloping Ghost: An Interview with Red Grange," *American Heritage*, December 1974.

Rice, Grantland. "Alumnus Football," *The Pittsburgh Press*, November 2, 1914.

Rothschild, Richard. "The Streak that Changed Football," http://sportsillustrated.cnn.com/2010/football/nfl/12/09/johnny.u/index.html.

Schwartz, Larry. "Galloping Ghost Scared Opponents," http://espn.go.com/sportscentury/features/00014213.html.

"Spot the Ball: ODOG Antarctica Football Match," www.peaceoneday.org/en/about/features/Spot-the-Ball.

Wyatt, Hugh. "Pro Football—The Early Days" www.coachwyatt.com/profootball_history1.htm.

## Websites

www.HickokSports.com
www.NFL.com
www.pro-football-reference.com
www.profootballhof.com

# IF YOU HAVE ENJOYED THIS BOOK, HALLMARK WOULD LOVE TO HEAR FROM YOU!

Please send your comments to:
Hallmark Book Feedback
P.O. BOX 419034
Mail Drop 215
Kansas City, MO 64141


Or e-mail us at:
booknotes@hallmark.com

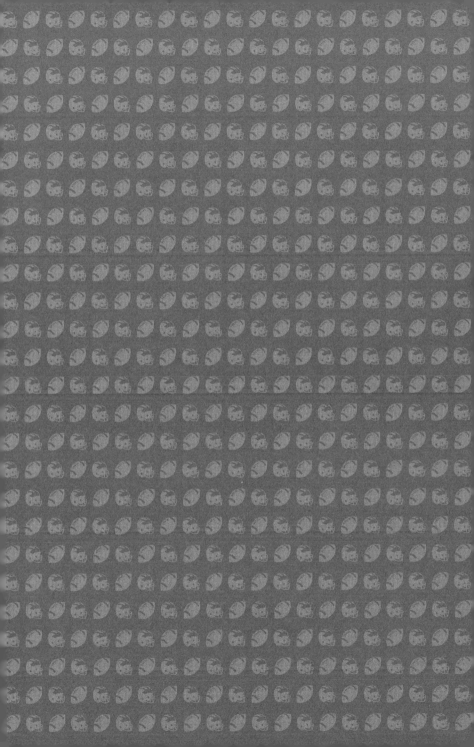